PRAISE FOR MA[...]

T0102053

Craft in the Real World

"This book is a gift to those writers who've felt the tilt of imbalanced power in a workshop, who've wondered whose rules they're following when they write and why, who've struggled to tell their stories within a narrow and restrictive tradition. With empathy and keen insight, Matthew Salesses delivers an unflinching critique of the pedagogy of creative writing's old guard—and models a way of studying and communicating craft that is self-aware, socially engaged, and thrillingly alive."

—ALEXANDRA KLEEMAN, author of *Intimations*

"This is exactly the book we need right now—a vital corrective to the myth that craft is a neutral, objective category unaffected by historical or cultural context. Matthew Salesses explores how beliefs about 'good' writing are profoundly marked by race, class, gender, sexuality, ability, and national identity; and he offers concrete strategies for liberating our classrooms and writing practices from the straight-white-male default gaze. I will recommend *Craft in the Real World* to every writer and teacher I know."

—LENI ZUMAS, author of *Red Clocks*

"With *Craft in the Real World*, Matthew Salesses has created a tremendous resource for anyone hoping to write fiction or teach fiction writing. It tackles head-on how craft has often been taught in the United States, and like the best teachers, it provides a practical path for much needed reform and improvement. This book teaches us how to ask better questions of our craft, our work, our workshops, and of each other. To have all of this pedagogical brilliance and thoughtfulness in one book is a gift."

—JENNINE CAPÓ CRUCET, author of
My Time Among the Whites

"Our students put their hearts on pages and they hand those pages to us. It's a profound act of trust and Matthew Salesses shows us how to be worthy of it. *Craft in the Real World* is required reading for writers, writing teachers, and everyone who loves language and what it can accomplish in our beautiful, complicated world."

—MEGAN STIELSTRA, author of
The Wrong Way to Save Your Life

Disappear Doppelgänger Disappear

"Inventive and profound, mordantly hilarious and wildly moving. Matthew Salesses is one of my all-time favorite writers." —LAURA VAN DEN BERG, author of
I Hold a Wolf by the Ears

CRAFT IN THE REAL WORLD

Rethinking Fiction Writing and Workshopping

MATTHEW SALESSES

CATAPULT
NEW YORK

Versions of some of these chapters were first published in:
Pleiades Magazine, Gulf Coast, Necessary Fiction, and *Electric Literature*

ISBN: 978-1-948226-80-6

Cover design by Nicole Caputo
Book design by Wah-Ming Chang

Library of Congress Control Number: 2020936778

Printed in the United States of America
10 9 8 7 6 5 4

CRAFT IN THE REAL WORLD

ALSO BY MATTHEW SALESSES

Disappear Doppelgänger Disappear

The Hundred-Year Flood: A Novel

I'm Not Saying, I'm Just Saying: A Novel

The Last Repatriate: A Novella

Our Island of Epidemics

Different Racisms: On Stereotypes, the Individual, and Asian American Masculinity

We Will Take What We Can Get

To all of my teachers and students,
especially M.L. and M.J.

CONTENTS

Preface   xiii

PART 1: FICTION IN THE REAL WORLD

"Pure Craft" Is a Lie   3

What Is Craft? 25 Thoughts   16

Audience, Theme, and Purpose   40

Redefining Craft Terms   49

. . . Tone   50

. . . Plot   55

. . . Conflict   59

. . . Character Arc and Story Arc   63

. . . Characterization   69

. . . Relatability   74

. . . Believability   79

. . . Vulnerability   84

. . . Setting   87

. . . Pacing   90

. . . Structure   94

An Example from East Asian and
Asian American Literature   99

PART 2: WORKSHOP IN THE REAL WORLD

"The Reader" vs. POC   113
Who Is at the Center of Workshop and
Who Should Be?   121
Alternative Workshops   130
Syllabus Example   144
Workshopping Incomplete Drafts   168
Against Page Limits   172
Four Things to Grade   176

APPENDIX: EXERCISES

Purpose-Oriented Writing Exercises   183
34 Revision Exercises   190

Works of Fiction Referenced   217
Further Bibliography   219
Acknowledgments   227

PREFACE

This book is a challenge to accepted models of craft and workshop, to everything from a character-driven plot to the "cone of silence," or "gag rule," that in a creative writing workshop silences the manuscript's author. The challenge is this: to take craft out of some imaginary vacuum (as if meaning in fiction is separate from meaning in life) and return it to its cultural and historical context. Race, gender, sexuality, etc. affect our lives and so must affect our fiction. Real-world context, and particularly what we do with that context, *is* craft.

Over a decade ago, I sat silently in an MFA workshop while mostly white writers discussed my race. I had decided not to name the race of any character, Asian American or otherwise—but the workshop demanded that the story inform "the reader" if my characters were like me, people of color. A common assumption lies behind this phenomenon: that no mention of race is supposed to mean a character is white. I didn't have to ask why the white writers in the room never identified the race of their white characters. I already knew why: they believed that white is literature's default. I just couldn't say so.

To name or not name a character's race is a matter of craft. To consider a character to be white unless stated otherwise is a matter of craft. Since this is a craft book, let's explore what exactly is at stake for the craft of fiction here. There are three possibilities:

1. If fiction dictates that a writer identify only the race of non-white characters, then craft is a tool used to normalize whiteness.
2. If race is a factor only in stories with characters of color, then craft must be different for fiction with characters of color than it is for fiction with white characters.
3. Otherwise, if any mention of race affects a story, then, like setting, race must be a part of any craft discussion.

Our current methods of teaching craft date back to at least 1936 and the creation of the Iowa Writers' Workshop, the first MFA program. The Workshop rose to prominence under the leadership (1941–1965) of Paul Engle, a white poet from Cedar Rapids, Iowa, who was invested in what scholar Eric Bennett calls "Iowa as the home of the free individual, of the poet at peace with democratic capitalism, of the novelist devoted to the contemporary outlines of liberty." (You will find more about this history later in the book.) In other words, the Workshop never meant craft to be neutral. Craft expressed certain artistic and social values that could be weaponized against the threat of Communism.

Craft is part of the history of Western empire that goes back even to the Ancient Greek and Roman empires, upon which American democratic values are based. We still talk about plot the way Aristotle wrote about it over two thousand years ago, when he argued that plot should be driven by character. When we continue to teach plot this way, we ignore both the many other kinds of plot found in literatures around the world and even the context of Aristotle's original complaint (he was fed up with the fate/god-driven plots popular with tragedians of his time).

What we call craft is in fact nothing more or less than a set of expectations. Those expectations are shaped by workshop, by reading, by awards and gatekeepers, by biases about whose stories matter and how they should be told. How we engage with craft expectations is what we can control as writers. The more we know about the context of those expectations, the more consciously we can engage with them.

These expectations are never neutral. They represent the values of the culturally dominant population: in America that means (straight, cis, able, upper-middle-class) white males. When craft is taught unreflexively, within a limited understanding of the canon, it reinforces narrow ideas about whose stories are important and what makes a story beautiful, moving, or good. We need to re-think craft and the teaching of it to better serve writers with increasingly diverse backgrounds, which means diverse ways of telling stories. Like in revision, the fiction writer must break down what she thinks she knows about her craft in order to liberate it.

This book is organized with the understanding that while some readers may read from start to finish, others may skip around according to their particular interests. For convenience, chapters are loosely collected in two parts, "Fiction in the Real World" and "Workshop in the Real World," though how we use craft and how we teach it are inseparable in a nation in which art has been institution-alized and many writers are supported financially and ideologically by colleges and universities. If you read this book from start to finish, you will find that some context is repeated as needed by particular chapters. In the appendix, you will find exercises that can be practiced alone or in the classroom.

This book is intended to begin further conversation— it should never be taken as an exhaustive or definitive resource. The conversation about power and craft must continue both in a more public context and in one's own personal context. Which is to say that while any writer benefits from encountering further possibilities, the lesson of this book is not that any writer should be able to use any cultural expectation no matter her identity position. An understanding that craft is cultural will also bring up issues of how to engage with craft appropriately, and those issues are inadequately addressed here. Likewise, this book does not present a representative range of perspectives, cultures, and narrative techniques, nor does it mean to. With luck, it will spark writers to find a place for themselves. I write and teach Asian American literature and will use it as an example throughout, but never as an example of what Asian American literature *should* do, only as an example of what Asian American literature *can* do and has done for me. Because of the lack of craft books that consider cultural context, *Craft in the Real World* primarily builds on two basic questions: Why do we limit our ideas about craft and workshop? and How do we start changing things?

That means, as much as possible, that this book will offer practical and practicable advice. To make craft accessible and inclusive, we must pull back the curtain on what craft is and does. In other words, dear reader, you will find no lightning bolts, no genius, no voices-in-my-head here. We must reject the mystification/ mythification of creative writing. The mystical writer uses the myth of his genius to gain power. He (since it is almost always a he) benefits from keeping up the illusions that he has natural talent and that writing cannot be taught. If writing is not beholden to culture, then he is free from the constraints of actually being a part of (or responsible to) the world in which he and his readers live.

Make no mistake—writing is power. What this fact should prompt us to ask is: What kind of power is it, where does it come from, and what does it mean?

If we take from Aristotle his idea of plot, for example, we should also remember that he believed art relied on slavery: slaves freed their masters to think and create. For the most part, writing has proved a privileged pursuit. To write for publication requires time, education, cultural fluency, and often financial solvency, connections, and a built-in audience. In order to become a writer at all, writing has to seem possible as a career path. Reading has to seem as valuable as work, friendships, dating, etc. Where does that sense of value come from?

Perhaps we know all about the privilege it takes to write. Yet somehow writers seem to forget that this context influences how we evaluate fiction, what we think of as *moving*, what we think of as *correct* or *well-written*. Literary criticism tells us that the Western novel is a product of the middle class. It is written by people in the middle class for an audience of people in the middle class. Novels are about social identity, mass production, the economy of art, and so on. But unlike in life, in fiction, class and race and gender, etc., are *choices*. That is, they are a part of craft. To become a better writer is to make conscious what may start out as unconscious.

This is all another way of saying that fiction can never be separated from its place in the world. Even the choice to write about something completely imaginary—elves and wizards—is a choice made by someone reacting to the world in which they live by fantasizing about another. It is also a choice about what kind of other world to fantasize— why elves and wizards rather than fox-spirits and ghosts?

This book will focus on literary fiction because its expectations are the expectations I know best. And like most readers, I actually enjoy having many of my expectations fulfilled and a few undermined or challenged. To meet expectations is not inherently bad. I love romantic comedies that stick close to the formula. Most of the TV we love is very formulaic. Most literary fiction is no different. It meets the expectations of a specific audience.

This book is against the idea of "finding" an audience and for the idea of writing toward the audience whose expectations matter to you. As writers we need to know that there are many different conventions—not just convention and experimentation—and we need to know where those conventions come from, and whom they serve, in order to know what and why and how to *mean*. If, as theory tells us, language always comes up short of representing experience, then how language evokes experience is as much about whose experience gets represented as it is about which words are chosen. Language evokes meaning *for someone*. Even a sentence like "She walked to the grocery store" requires some cultural context. What a grocery store is like, what challenges walking presents, perhaps an entire setting can be called to mind in the gaps between words and the way those gaps are filled in by a reader's personal and cultural assumptions.

When the "traditional" creative writing workshop, in which the author submits a manuscript to a group of peers and listens silently, began at Iowa, it was developed with shared assumptions in mind. The workshop was made up of white males reading white male fiction, as students and especially as instructors. In this world only does the "gag rule" make some sense, in that it forced men used to being heard to stop and listen to their likely audience. But the world has moved on. The traditional workshop does not work without shared assumptions. It doesn't work if some of the writers in the room have different audiences or expectations—as in the workshop where I was told to race characters of color. At best, it pressures the least normative writers to make fiction that is "likeable" and generalizable to the most normative audience. Non-normative experience becomes exoticized or unspecific, something extra rather than something foundational.

If this idea of craft persists, it is because workshop pedagogy (as Kelly Ritter and Stephanie Vanderslice argued back in 2005) is largely shaped by "lore," by writers teaching what they learned as students, rather than by pedagogical theory or intersectional criticism. What does the traditional workshop offer? One common refrain is that writers learn most from hearing what they haven't yet realized about their own work. And this is an important aspect of workshop, just not one that is actually best served by silence. Imagine, for example, a conversation about gardening in which other gardeners look at your garden and tell you about it without allowing you to talk about your attempts to grow it. This conversation is at best underinformed. It is likely to mislead. It could easily end up harmful to both the garden and even the gardener's desire to garden, especially if the other gardeners have experience in a different kind of garden, or with different plants, or a different climate, or soil, etc.

In other words, the traditional model does not work in the real world. The "gag rule" tells those who are silenced that in order to speak they must speak with an acceptable voice. Especially when the workshop focuses on form and avoids content, it says to the silent author: *You own your story but not how you get to tell it or whom you get to tell it to.* Your story must be framed so that the majority can read via their own lens.

The later chapters in this book will expand on the dangers of traditional workshop, the unbalanced and often hurtful power dynamics it mimics and perpetuates, the stultification of different kinds of craft, the hide-and-seek game created by the term "the reader," and ways to teach craft with more cultural understanding and sensitivity. As Laura Mulvey said about pleasure in film and the male gaze, pleasure or interest in workshop is based on how one group "sees" the work, and that group's gaze is built into the model. The gaze persists even without the group to do the looking—just as the male gaze persists in film even when the film is watched by someone who does not identify as male. We must take apart the whole model.

If we are trying, through workshop, to see our own work better, to re-see (as in revision), then with which gaze are we re-seeing? Workshop should be a place that helps a writer see and re-see for herself. The goal of workshop should be to provide the tools a writer will use long after the workshop disbands. Has it instead become a place in which we teach writers how to *be* seen? Does it encourage the false equivalence of "the reader" as the workshop?

Workshop has created many axioms: "show, don't tell," "write what you know," "kill your darlings," etc. Writers have pushed back against those axioms, but we must also push back against the context that creates them, that nurtures them and passes them on. If not, we simply recreate the same exceptions within the same culturally defined argument we were taught to engage in. Whole other traditions of writing become only rule-breaking, boundary-crossing. Some of us have larger arguments at stake, arguments often about the bounds of the argument themselves, of what is and is not normal, good, beautiful.

A workshop should not participate in the binding but in freeing the writer from the culturally regulated boundaries of what it is possible to say and how it is possible to say it.

Part 1

FICTION IN THE REAL WORLD

"PURE CRAFT" IS A LIE

Like many creative writing instructors, I teach my students that it can be to their advantage in fiction to use the dialogue tags "say" and "ask" instead of less common tags like "commented" or "queried." This is a strategy I myself was taught. The usual reasoning goes like this: the tags "say" and "ask" are effectively "invisible" to readers, so they take the reader's focus off the tag and put it on who is talking. Most of the time, the main purpose of a dialogue tag is to indicate who has spoken. (Tags also provide rhythm and other benefits, but let's focus on this main purpose.) I tell my students that if the main purpose of a particular tag is not who is speaking but *how* the character speaks, such as in a shout or a whisper, then those dialogue tags ("she shouted," "they whispered") become useful for the very fact that they are not "invisible." Readers are meant to register the way of speaking as much or more than who is doing it. When writers use "say" or "ask," it isn't to get readers to register the fact that something is said or asked—the dialogue already makes this obvious.

I believe this advice to be useful and true. I also know that it is cultural. We read "say" and "ask" as invisible terms not, of course, because they are invisible, and not because of their meaning—"commented" and "queried" would do in this regard—but because we have read other books that also use "say" and "ask." We read the words "say" and "ask" *a lot*, so much that we barely notice them.

To be clear, if every writer in America started using the word "queried," then American readers would start to treat "queried" as invisible. That is the influence of culture. Our exposure to culture is what makes our advice on dialogue tags advisable. To learn craft is to learn how to use cultural expectations to your advantage.

Craft works best, then, when a writer and reader share the same cultural background. If a writer were to use "ask" in a culture where "queried" is the invisible term, then "ask" would draw attention to itself—it would lose its value as invisible. A reader who picks up her first literary novel in English will often question why an author repetitively writes "say" and "ask," instead of changing it up with synonyms. Many primary schools teach children to avoid repetition (one real benefit is to improve children's vocabulary). I've had the experience of assigning Hemingway to ESL readers, thinking of his simplicity, only for them to ask why Hemingway is such a bad writer. Why the hell does he keep using the same dialogue tags over and over? Why doesn't he know any bigger words?

I use the example of dialogue tags for its relative

straightforwardness, but cultural expectations also apply to how we characterize, why some characters are called "unsympathetic" and others are not, how we plot by causation and agency rather than by coincidence, how we emphasize conflict, how we expect characters to change or at least actively fail to change, etc. If not everything about fiction is cultural (though how could it not be, when language is cultural), certainly any aspect of craft that relies on shared meanings relies on shared culture. This is why aspiring writers should read a lot, and why artists learn art history, and why certain fiction gets grouped together under terms like "Modernism" or "Fantasy."

Here's a quick thought experiment. Imagine a writer from a culture that uses "query" enrolls in a creative writing workshop in our "ask" culture. How much would the repetition of "queried" frustrate the workshop? The writer might even be convinced to use "ask" from then on.

What's the problem with that? To switch to using "ask" is to switch audiences. "Ask" is not for readers from the writer's "query" culture but for the workshop. Suddenly the writer has changed allegiances.

We must be careful not to frame craft as prescription or even guidelines without first making it clear where those guidelines come from and whom they benefit. In many workshops, in many craft books, the dominance of one tradition of craft, serving one particular audience (white, middle-class, straight, able, etc.), is essentially literary imperialism, a term that should make us wary of the danger especially to emerging minority and marginalized voices.

Here plenty of writers will feign queasiness over any introduction of politics or literary theory. There is, of course, a kind of writer who believes art is free from the rest of the world, as if he does not live and read and write in that world. There is also a kind of writer who believes that human experience is universal, so his experience is enough to know everyone else's. What's the big deal, these privileged writers will ask: Why not encourage writers to reach a "wide" "mainstream" audience? Even if they want to experiment, they should know tradition first.

In other words: "You have to know the rules in order to break them."

These tired arguments get trotted out whenever writers are asked to take more responsibility for their positions in the world. But reading and writing are not done in a vacuum. What people read and write affects how they act in the world. If writers really believe that art is important to actual life, then the responsibilities of actual life are the responsibilities of art. The argument that one should know the rules before breaking them is really an argument about who gets to make the rules, whose rules get to be the norms and determine the exceptions. To teach the writer from a "query" culture to use "ask" is not to teach her how to write *better* but to teach her *whose*

writing is better. Writing that follows nondominant cultural standards is often treated as if it is "breaking the
rules," but why one set of rules and not another? What is
official always has to do with power.

To sum up, what we are telling the writer from a
"query" culture who learns to write "ask" is (a) she must
either write to people from our culture, instead of hers,
or learn how to write to people from our culture if she
wants to write to people from hers; (b) she should accept
our normal as her normal; and (c) she is at a disadvantage
toward the shared learning goals, since writers from our
culture don't have to learn new norms; they only have to
recognize the norms they already understand.

Now extend this hypothetical situation to real people
who, for whatever reason, are less familiar with or less
invested in the cultural expectations of the dominant
literature. I'll give you another example, one many creative writing instructors are familiar with—a workshop
in which most people want to write "literary" fiction, but
Student X and maybe a few others want to write "high
fantasy." I am not entirely versed in fantasy, but I am
versed in this situation. The people who prefer literary
fiction likely have read a lot of literary fiction and less fantasy. The people who prefer fantasy have likely read a lot
of fantasy and less literary fiction. (These terms are used
too sweepingly here, with distinctions I don't endorse, but
let's put that aside for the sake of the example.)

The instructor sets out to teach characterization,

assigns a literary story with "complex, three-dimensional characters," and says something like, characters should not be "types." If I am Student X, the hypothetical fantasy-writer, I might find that my instructor's words are not supported by my experience. In many of the books I read, characters are "types" and could not be otherwise. An elf who does not act like an elf is a poorly written character. The term "type" might even strike me as a strange way to refer to non-"complex" characters. Why shouldn't an elf-like elf be complex? Plus, the literary story the instructor assigned as a model bores me, and I don't see why it has any value other than by being literary. Its superiority to everything high fantasy seems taken for granted by the workshop.

Do I raise my hand to object or even to ask questions? It is possible that my objections will lead to an interesting discussion about what a "type" is and does. But it is also possible that I will feel mocked or attacked or at least condescended to. Likely I won't say anything at all. After all, I am already expending a lot of mental energy trying to keep up with what my instructor means by "types" and what makes something "literary" or not, while my classmates seem to require very little explanation. The whole idea of workshop is terrifying enough without the added pressure of coming off as ignorant, especially when I will have to face my classmates' criticism in silence anyway.

It is true that many instructors would want the interesting discussion that might arise if the fantasy writer voices her objections. But this (hypothetical) class is already set up to make a fair discussion difficult. There is a lot of bias in the room—most of the writers already prefer literary fiction, and everyone has read a literary story as the example text, and the instructor is better understood by the literary writers and vice versa, and the instructor is respected *as* a literary writer. How can Student X catch up when the gap between her knowledge of literary conventions and the other students' knowledge only widens as new lessons continue to build on past lessons?

I have been in this kind of workshop both as a student and a professor. An open-minded workshop leader may indeed encourage interesting discussion and, as many professors would argue, Student X may indeed learn to write better fantasy by incorporating literary craft (and vice versa). But none of this changes the fact that everything is stacked against Student X from go. Even if Student X's instructor *wants* to teach her to write literary fiction (not my goal, but a goal I have often heard stated by MFA professors), that option is never fully made available to her. If Student X never realizes that she is learning cultural values, then what she learns is that her knowledge of the world isn't useful in a craft discussion and needs to be discarded.

The literary writers enjoy a lot of privilege in this workshop compared to Student X. The instructor teaches mostly to them; they have a foundation of knowledge with which to immediately process lessons; they are invested in that knowledge and the culture that produces it; and they are invested in producing more of that culture, for an audience similarly invested. The rich get richer.

The writer with different cultural values has to learn more than the terms and sayings of literary craft. She has to learn a whole new value system, a whole new tradition. If she believes that she must learn that tradition's rules before she can break them, then she has to become a part of that tradition before she can figure out whether or not its craft will be useful to her old tradition.

So much for the neutrality of genre. Now imagine a workshop of twelve people who are *all* interested in "literary" writing. Three of them are writers of color. Imagine that the readings are all by white writers, and the instructor is white. Imagine that this instructor keeps insisting that fiction is not ideological.

I have been in that workshop too, many times. Of course, only as a student.

Writers of color in a workshop where the craft values are implicitly white, or LGBT writers in a workshop where the craft values are straight and cis, or women writers in a workshop where the craft values are patriarchal, and so on, are regularly told to "know the rules before they can break them." They are rarely told that these rules are more than "just craft" or "pure craft," that rules are always cultural. The spread of craft starts to feel and work like colonization.

Let us look at one final example, focusing on the use of sensory details. Fiction writers are often taught the three following strategies for using sensory details in their stories:

1. Choose "striking" or "lasting" or "unusual" (or so forth) details.
2. Leave out unnecessary or "common" details.
3. Defamiliarize the familiar.

Imagine that one of the three writers of color in the workshop submits a story about characters of color. For the purpose of the example, we will imagine that the workshop was taught the three strategies above and is supposed to address them in the manuscript. Let's go over some typical comments. Since these are comments I have heard and/or experienced firsthand, pretend the story is about Korean Americans in Korea. We'll explore two separate possibilities: one in which the writer takes the advice of cultural craft, and one in which the writer resists that craft. For convenience, let's start with the first two strategies and come back to the third later.

Say the writer has taken the first two pieces of advice. He has included what he thinks are striking details—the fish a man is taking home on the subway, the man's incorrectly buttoned coat, the smell of unwashed bodies, the slickness of the bodies pressed close—all details which will be important to some kind of plot concerning the man with the fish—and he has left out other details that are unnecessary to the story.

In this scenario, it would not be surprising to hear the workshop say that the writer has not done the things that he in fact did: i.e. including unusual details and leaving out unnecessary details. The other writers might suggest he include details like—an extreme example—passengers eating kimchi in their box lunches. This seems like a reasonable suggestion to them because the strategies for using sensory details assume a white audience and white cultural norms. In other words, the writer should be addressing white Americans who may have experienced the smell of unwashed bodies but would be "struck" by the "vivid" details of the smell of kimchi or so forth. There might even be a white American in the workshop who speaks up to say he's been to Korea and goes on to give some examples of what he found unusual.

As an opposite scenario, say the writer *resists* the craft lessons and, following other writers of color he has read (and writing against stories in which white expats in Asia eat exotified food on the lunar new year, etc.), tries to include details that would be common and recognizable to a Korean American audience. Details, for instance, like how the man with the fish can tell by the protagonist's clothes that he's a gyopo. Maybe the writer includes these recognizable details because he knows how little fiction there is about people like him and he believes that representation is important. In this workshop, the other writers might ask him to define "gyopo" if it is supposed to be a striking detail. They might complain that if it is not a striking detail, the writer should cut it. They might complain that the word is not clear to them, or that if it is supposed to be a common word, the writer should cut it. They might say that "the spell of the story was broken" for them when they encountered a word they didn't know and couldn't figure out from context clues. Again, these would be appropriate responses—*if* the point of craft is to meet the expectations of an audience who is not like the writer.

Lastly, let's talk about defamiliarization. If the writer tried to familiarize rather than defamiliarize, the responses would be similar to those in the paragraph above. If the writer tries to defamiliarize, to *take* the craft advice—say he defamiliarizes the familiar lunch box by describing it as a little square house with a room for each side dish—it wouldn't be surprising to hear the workshop object. They might say they can't understand what the square house of side dishes is. They might even encourage the writer not to defamiliarize, since common details of Korean culture are already unfamiliar enough for them. The writer will likely end up either in conflict or simply in confusion, not knowing (because the workshop never says it) that the criticism is not of his craft, but of his cultural position.

I began this essay in response to a writer friend asking why writers of color don't write "pure craft" essays, rather than craft essays about race. This essay is a way of answering her question with a question: Why do we believe there is any such thing as "pure craft"? When writers identify race and gender and sexuality, etc., as central concerns of writing, it isn't because they have nothing to say about pacing or space breaks. They are doing the hard work other writers avoid, in order to shed light on the nature of craft itself.

They are:

a.   reacting to a history of craft as "just craft" and even trying to correct it,

b.   catching up writers outside the dominant culture by teaching the cultural context that goes mostly unexamined, and

c.   making sure that they do not participate in the erasure of their own difference.

The way we tell stories has real consequences on the way we interpret meaning in our everyday lives. The books I read as a child, about children who find they are actually heirs to some magical kingdom, of course affected the way I thought about my adoption, which of course affects the way I think about plot and character and conflict and so on. Craft is not innocent or neutral. When I participate in the sharing and changing of craft,

I can only do so by acknowledging my own attraction to certain cultural conventions. Culture stands behind what makes many craft moves "work" or not, and *for whom* they work. Writers need to understand their real-world relationship to craft in order to understand their relationship to their audience and to their writing's place in the world. There's a lot of work left to do to open up craft to writers beyond the cis, straight, white, able, middle-class (etc.) literary establishment, and there is no "pure" way of doing that work. There is only our engagement with culture.

WHAT IS CRAFT? 25 THOUGHTS

1.

Craft is a set of expectations.

2.

Expectations are not universal; they are standardized. It is like what we say about wine or espresso: we acquire "taste." With each story we read, we draw on and contribute to our knowledge of what a story is or should be. This is true of cultural standards as fundamental as whether to read from left to right or right to left, just as it is true of more complicated context such as how to appreciate a sentence like "She was absolutely sure she hated him," which relies on our expectation that stating a person's certainty casts doubt on that certainty as well as our expectation that fictional hatred often turns into attraction or love.

Our appreciation then *relies on* but also *reinforces* our expectations.

What expectations, however, are we really talking about here?

In her book *Immigrant Acts*, theorist Lisa Lowe argues that the novel regulates cultural ideas of identity, nationhood, gender, sexuality, race, and history. Lowe suggests that Western psychological realism, especially the *bildungsroman*/coming-of-age novel, has tended toward stories about an individual reincorporated into society—an outsider finds his place in the world, though not without loss. Other writers and scholars share Lowe's reading. Examples abound: In *Jane Eyre*, Jane marries Rochester. In *Pride and Prejudice*, Elizabeth Bennet marries Mr. Darcy. In *The Age of Innocence*, Newland Archer, after some hesitation, marries May Welland. (There is a lot of marriage.) In *The Great Gatsby*, Nick Carraway returns to the Midwest and Daisy Buchanan returns to her husband.

Some of these protagonists end up happy and some unhappy, but all end up incorporated into society. A common craft axiom states that by the end of a story, a protagonist must either change or fail to change. These novels fulfill this expectation. In the end, it's not only the characters who find themselves trapped by societal norms. It's the novels.

3.

But expectations are not a bad thing. In a viral craft talk on YouTube, author Kurt Vonnegut graphs several archetypal (Western) story structures, such as "Man in a Hole" (a protagonist gets in trouble and then gets out of it) and

Cinderella (which Vonnegut jokes automatically earns an author a million dollars). The archetypes are recognizable to us the way that beats in a romantic comedy are recognizable to us—a meet-cute, mutual dislike, the realization of true feelings, consummation, a big fight, some growing up, and a reunion (often at the airport). The fulfillment of expectations is pleasurable. Part of the fun of Vonnegut's talk is that he shows us how well we already know certain story types and how our familiarity with them doesn't decrease, maybe only increases, our fondness for them. Any parent knows that a child's favorite stories are the stories she has already heard. Children like to know what is coming. It reduces their anxiety, validates their predictions, and leaves them able to learn from other details. Research suggests that children learn more from a story they already know. What they do not learn is precisely: other stories.

Craft is also about omission. What rules and archetypes standardize are models that are easily generalizable to accepted cultural preferences. What doesn't fit the model is othered. What is our responsibility to the other? In his book *The Hero with a Thousand Faces*, Joseph Campbell famously theorized a "monomyth" story shape common to all cultures. In reality, his theory is widely dismissed as reductionist—far more selective than universal and unjustly valuing similarity over difference. It has been especially criticized for the way its focus on the "hero's journey" dismisses stories like the heroine's journey or other stories in which people do not set off to conquer and return with booty (knowledge and/or spirituality and/or riches and/or love objects). It is important to recognize Campbell's investment in masculinity as universal.

Craft is the history of which kind of stories have typically held power—and for whom—so it also is the history of which stories have typically been omitted. That we have certain expectations for what a story is or should include means we also have certain expectations for what a story isn't or shouldn't include. Any story relies on negative space, and a tradition relies on the negative space of history. The ability for a reader to fill in white space relies on that reader having seen what *could* be there. Some readers are asked to stay always, only, in the negative. To wield craft responsibly is to take responsibility for absence.

4.

In "A Journey Into Speech," Michelle Cliff writes about how she had to break from accepted craft in order to tell her story. Cliff grew up under colonial rule in Jamaica and was taught the "King's English" in school. To write well was to write in one specific mode. She went to graduate school and even published her dissertation, but when she started to write directly about her experience, she found that it could not be represented by the kind of language and forms she had learned.

In order to include her own experience, Cliff says she

had to reject a British "cold-blooded dependence on logical construction." She mixed vernacular with the King's English, mixed Caribbean stories and ways of storytelling with British. She wrote in fragments, to embody her fragmentation. She reclaimed the absences that formed the way she spoke and thought, that created the "split-consciousness" she lived with.

To own her writing—I am paraphrasing—was to own herself. This is craft.

5.

Craft is both much more and much less than we're taught it is.

6.

In his book on post–World War II MFA programs, Eric Bennett documents how the Iowa Writers' Workshop, the first place to formalize the education of creative writing, fundraised on claims that it would spread American values of freedom, of creative writing and art in general as "the last refuge of the individual." The Workshop popularized an idea of craft as non-ideological, but its claims should make clear that individualism is itself an ideology. (It shouldn't surprise us that apolitical writing has long been a political stance.) If we can admit by now that history is about who has had the power to write history, we should be able to admit the same of craft. Craft is about who has the power to write stories, what stories are historicized and who historicizes them, who gets to write literature and who folklore, whose writing is important and to whom, in what context. This is the process of standardization. If craft is teachable, it is because standardization is teachable. These standards must be challenged and disempowered. Too often craft is taught only as what has already been taught before.

7.

In the West, fiction is inseparable from the project of the individual. Craft as we know it from Aristotle to E. M. Forster to John Gardner rests on the premise that a work of creative writing represents an individual creator, who, as Ezra Pound famously put it, "makes it new." Not on the premise that Thomas King describes in *The Truth About Stories: A Native Narrative*: that any engagement with speaking is an engagement with listening, that to tell a story is always to retell it, and that no story has behind it an individual. Each "chapter" of King's book, in fact, begins and ends almost the same way and includes a quote from another Native writer.

Audre Lorde puts it this way: "There are no new ideas. There are only new ways of making them felt, *of examining what our ideas really mean*." (My italics.)

It is clear in an oral tradition that individual creation is impossible—the authors of the *Thousand and One Nights*, the "Beowulf poet," Homer, were all engaging with the expectations their stories had accrued over many tellings.

Individualism does not free one from cultural expectations; it *is* a cultural expectation. Fiction does not "make
it new;" it makes it *felt*. Craft does not separate the author
from the real world.

When I was in graduate school, a famous white writer
defended Joseph Conrad's *Heart of Darkness* (whose craft
was famously criticized by author Chinua Achebe for the
racist use of Africans as objects and setting rather than as
characters) by claiming that the book should be read for
craft, not race. Around the same time, another famous
white writer gave a public talk in a sombrero about the
freedom to appropriate. Thomas King, on the contrary,
respects the shared responsibility of storytelling and
warns us that to tell a story one way can "cure," while to
tell it another can injure.

Craft is never neutral. Craft is the cure or injury that
can be done in our shared world when it isn't acknowl-
edged that there are different ways that world is felt.

8.

Since craft is always about expectations, two questions to ask
are: Whose expectations? and Who is free to break them?

Audre Lorde again: "The master's tools will never dismantle the master's house."

Lorde presents a difficult problem for people who
understand that freedom is never general but always freedom *for someone*: how to free oneself from oppression while
using the language of one's oppressors? This is a problem

Lorde perhaps never fully "solved." Maybe it has no solution, but it can't be dismissed. When we are first handed craft, we are handed the master's tools. We are told we must learn the rules before we can dismantle them. We build the master's house, and then we look to build houses of our own, but we are given no new tools. We must find them or we must work around the tools we have.

To wield craft is always to wield a tool that already exists. Author Trinh Minh-ha writes that even the expectation of "clarity" is an expectation of what is "correct" and/or "official" language. Clear to whom? Take round and flat characters. In *Toward the Decolonization of African Literature*, authors Chinweizu, Onwuchekwa Jemie, and Ihechukwu Madubuike complain that African literature is unfairly criticized by Western critics as lacking round characters. E. M. Forster's original definition of roundness is "capable of surprising in a convincing way." Chinweizu et al. point out that this definition is clear evidence that roundness comes not from the author's words but from the audience's reading. One reader from one background might be convincingly surprised while another reader from another background might be unsurprised and/or unconvinced by the same character.

Whom are we writing for?

9.

Expectations belong to an audience. To use craft is to engage with an audience's bias. Like freedom, craft is always craft *for someone*. Whose expectations does a writer prioritize? Craft says something about who deserves their story told. Who has agency and who does not. What is worthy of action and what description. Whose bodies are on display. Who changes and who stays the same. Who controls time. Whose world it is. Who holds meaning and who gives it.

Nobel Prize–winning author Toni Morrison suggests in *Playing in the Dark* that the craft of American fiction is to use Black people and images and culture as symbols, as tools. In other words, the craft of American fiction is the tool that names who the master is. To signify light as good, as we are taught to do from our first children's stories, is to signify darkness as bad—and in this country lightness and darkness will always be tied to a racialized history of which people are people and which people are tools. To engage in craft is always to engage in a hierarchy of symbolization (and to not recognize a hierarchy is to hide it). Who can use that hierarchy, those tools? Not I, says Morrison. And so she sets off to find other craft.

10.

In his book *The Art of the Novel*, Czech author Milan Kundera rejects psychological realism as the tradition of the European novel. He offers an alternate history that begins with *Don Quixote* and goes through Franz Kafka. He offers this history in order to make a claim about craft, because he knows that craft must come from somewhere. Contrary to psychological realism's focus on individual agency, Kundera's alternate craft says that the main cause of action in a novel is the world's "naked" force.

Kundera wants to decenter internal causation (character-driven plot) and (re)center external causation (such as an earthquake or fascism or God). He insists that psychological realism is no "realer" than the bureaucratic world Kafka presents in which individuals have little or no agency and everything is a function of the system. (This is also a claim about how to read history.) Only our expectations of what realism is/should be make us classify one type of fiction (which by definition is not "real") as realer than another. Any novel, for Kundera, is about a possible way of "being in the world," and Kafka's bureaucracy came true in the Czech Republic in a way that individual agency did not.

Another advocate of Kafka's brand of "realism" is the author Julio Cortázar. Cortázar is usually considered a fabulist or magical realist. Yet in a series of lectures collected in *Literature Class*, he categorizes his own and other "fantastic" stories as simply more inclusive realities. He uses his story "The Island at Noon" as an example, in which a character dives into the ocean to save a drowning man, only to find that the man is himself. The story ends with a fisherman walking onto the beach we have just seen, alone "as always." The swimmer and the drowner were never there. Cortázar says this story represents a real experience of time in which, like a daydream, it becomes impossible to tell what is real and what is not. Time, fate, magic—these are forces beyond human agency that to Cortázar allow literature to "make reality more real."

In *Toward the Decolonization of African Literature*, Chinweizu et al. encourage African writers to remember African traditions of storytelling. They identify four conventions from a tradition of incoporating the fantastic into everyday life: (1) spirit beings have a non-human trait that gives them away, such as floating; (2) if a human visits the spiritland, it involves a dangerous border-crossing; (3) spirits have agency and can possess humans; and (4) spirits are not subject to human concepts of time and space.

Craft tells us how to see the world.

11.

The Iowa Writers' Workshop established craft's current focus on style and form, writes Eric Bennett, a focus which also conveniently

> served four related agendas: (1) it overthrew the domination of totalitarian manipulation (if Soviet) or commercial manipulation (if American) by being irreducibly individualistic; (2) it facilitated the creation of an ideologically informed canon [of dead white men] on ostensibly apolitical grounds; (3) it provided a modernist means

to make literature feel transcendent for the ages [rather than tied to time and place]; and (4) it gave reading and writing a new semblance of difficulty, a pitch of rigor appropriate for the college or graduate school classroom.

In other words, it made literature easy to fundraise for, and easy to teach.

12.

We have come to teach plot as a string of causation in which the protagonist's desires move the action forward. The craft of fiction has come to adopt the terms of Freytag's triangle, which were meant to apply to drama, and of Aristotle's poetics, which were meant to apply to Greek tragedy. Exposition, inciting incident, rising action, climax, falling action, resolution, denouement. But to think of plot and story shape in this way is cultural and represents the dominance of a specific cultural tradition.

In contrast, Chinese, Korean, and Japanese stories have developed from a four-act, rather than a three- or five-act structure: in Japanese it is called kishotenketsu (ki: introduction; sho: development; ten: twist; ketsu: reconciliation). Western fiction can often be boiled down to A wants B and C gets in the way of it. I draw this shape for my students:

A———>B and A—C   B

This kind of story shape is inherently conflict-based, perhaps also inherently male (as author Jane Alison puts it: "Something that swells and tautens until climax, then collapses? Bit masculo-sexual, no?"). In East Asian fiction, the twist (ten) is not confrontation but surprise, something that reconfigures what its audience thinks the story is "about." For example, a man puts up a flyer of a missing dog, he hands out flyers to everyone on the street, a woman appears and asks whether her dog has been found, they look for the dog together. The change in this kind of story is in the audience's understanding or attention rather than what happens. Like African storytellers, Asian storytellers are often criticized for what basically amounts to addressing a different audience's different expectations—Asian fiction gets labeled "undramatic" or "plotless" by Western critics.

The Greek tragedians were likewise criticized by Aristotle. In his *Poetics*, Aristotle does not just put forward an early version of Western craft (one closely tied to his philosophical project of the individual) but also puts down many of his contemporaries, tragedians for whom action is driven by the interference of the gods (in the form of coincidence) rather than from a character's internal struggle. It is from Aristotle that Westerners get the cultural distaste for *deus ex machina*, which was more like the fashion of his time. Aristotle's dissent went forward as the norm.

13.

Craft, like the self, is made by culture and reflects culture, and can develop to resist and reshape culture if it is sufficiently examined and enough work is done to unmake expectations and replace them with new ones. (As Aristotle did by writing the first craft book.)

We are constantly telling stories—about who we are, about every person we see, hear, hear about—and when we don't know something, we fill in the gaps with parts of stories we've told or heard before. Stories are always only representations. To tell a story about a person based on her clothes, or the color of her skin, or the way she talks, or her body—is to subject her to a set of cultural expectations. In the same way, to tell a story based on a character-driven plot or a moment of epiphany or a three-act structure leading to a character's change is to subject story to cultural expectations. To wield craft morally is not to pretend that those expectations can be met innocently or artfully without ideology, but to engage with the problems ideology presents and creates.

In my research for this book, I found various authors (mostly foreign) asking how it is that we have forgotten that character is made up, that it isn't real or universal. Kundera points out that we have bought unreflexively into conventions that say (a) that a writer should give the maximum information about a character's looks and speech, (b) that backstory contains motivation, and (c) that writers somehow do not have control over their characters. Nobel Prize winner Orhan Pamuk, in *The Naive and Sentimental Novelist*, complains that creative writing programs make it seem as if characters are autonomous beings who have their own voices, when in fact character is a "historical construct . . . we choose to believe in." To Pamuk, a character isn't even formed by an individual personality but by the particular situation and context the author needs her for. When it's all made up, he suggests, character is more nurture than nature. If fiction encourages a certain way that a character should be understood or read, then of course this way must influence and be influenced by the way we understand and read each other.

14.

To really engage with craft is to engage with how we know each other. Craft is inseparable from identity. Craft does not exist outside of society, outside of culture, outside of power. In the world we live in, and write in, craft must reckon with the implications of our expectations for what stories should be—with, as Lorde says, what our ideas really mean.

15.

Consider the example of the Chinese literary tradition, which we will get to later in the book. Western critics have generally called traditional Chinese fiction formless. Yet Chinese critic Zheng Zhenduo, who studies the

Chinese novel's historical trajectory, says one characteristic of Chinese fiction is that it is "water-tight," by which he means that it is structurally sound. They are describing the same fiction but different expectations.

While Western narrative comes from romantic and epic tradition, Chinese narrative comes from a tradition of gossip and street talk. Chinese fiction has always challenged historical record and accepted versions of "reality." Western storytelling developed from a tradition of oral performances meant to recount heroic deeds for an audience of the ruling class. Like Thomas King, author Ming Dong Gu, in his book *Chinese Theories of Fiction*, describes writing as something more like "transmission" than like "creation." More collective and less individual.

16.

Chinese American author Gish Jen claims in *Tiger Writing* that her fiction combines Western and Eastern craft. She makes a case for an Asian American storytelling that mixes the "independent" and "interdependent" self: the individual speaker vs. the collective speaker, internal agency vs. external agency.

The difficulty for Jen in her fiction was not in finding it a Western audience but in representing her Chinese values. As Jen writes, "existing schema are powerful." Growing up with American and European fiction, she struggled to represent her culture and self. The kind of agency a Western protagonist has was compelling to her—she describes it almost as a seduction—being so different from her family life. *Tiger Writing* actually begins with Jen analyzing her father's memoir, which is mostly family history and only gets around to himself in the final third. The suggestion is that family history, the ancestral home, their immigration to America, is exactly what defines her father, rather than any individual characteristic. Jen compares the memoir to a Chinese teapot, which unlike an American teapot is worth much more used than new, prized for how many teas have already been made in it, so that the flavor of a new tea mixes with the flavors before it.

17.

"Know your audience" is craft. Language has meaning because it has meaning *for someone*. Meaning and audience do not exist without one another. A word spoken to no one, not even the self, has no meaning because it has no one to hear it. It has no purpose.

Chinweizu, Jemie, and Madubuike employ the metaphor of an artist's sketch. Responding to Western critics who claim African fiction has too little description and weak characterization, they compare the relationship between craft and expectation to the relationship between a sketch and its evocation of a picture. "It perhaps needs to be stressed that the adequacy of a sketch depends upon its purpose, its context, and also upon what its beholders accept as normal or proper." In other words, "the writer's primary audience" may find the sketch enough to evoke the picture even if the European audience cannot. It shouldn't be the writer's concern to satisfy an audience who is not hers.

African fiction is written for Africans—what is easier to understand than that? Not that other people can't read it, but, as Chinweizu et al. tell us, it might take "time and effort and a sloughing off of their racist superiority complexes and imperialist arrogance" to appreciate it.

When the *Thousand and One Nights* is translated into English, translators often cut stories. The *Nights* is a story about storytelling, full of framed narratives, stories within stories within stories. Like Chinese fiction, it is often accused of the opposite sins of African fiction—of having too many digressions and extraneous parts. Part of the necessity of abridgment is that the *Nights* is extremely long, and part is that different versions of the *Nights* include different groups of stories—it might be impossible to include every story or to know what a complete version of the *Nights* would even look like, as every telling is a retelling—but stories that get cut out as extraneous are never actually pointless. Author Ulrich Marzolph argues convincingly that repetition of similar stories and themes and motifs is not a failure of craft but "a highly effective narrative technique for linking new and unknown tales to a web of tradition the audience shares." Children learn the most from stories they already know.

Similar abridgments occur in translations of traditional Chinese fiction. Again, these are often cases of translators misrepresenting the audience. In Chinese fiction, repetitions and digressions like those in the *Nights* are called "Casual Touches" and are a sign of mastery. According to author Jianan Qian, it takes a very good writer to be able to add "seemingly unrelated details . . . here and there effortlessly to stretch and strengthen a story's meanings." What is considered "good writing" is a matter of who is reading it.

18.

There are many crafts, and one way the teaching of craft fails is to teach craft as if it is one.

19.

Author Jennifer Riddle Harding writes about what she calls "masked narrative" in African American fiction, in which Black authors wrote to two audiences at the same time: a white audience they needed in order to have a career and a Black audience who would be able to understand a second, "hidden" meaning through context clues that rely on cultural knowledge. As an example, Harding analyzes a story by Charles W. Chesnutt about a white-presenting woman who wants to know who her mother is, and a Black caretaker who allows the woman to think her mother was white—though a Black audience would realize that the caretaker *is* the actual mother.

Different expectations guide different readings. "The black story had to look like a white story," writes the author Raymond Hedin, while also speaking to a Black audience via the same words.

In other words, the plot of external causation that Kundera would like to return to never disappeared; it was simply underground. In America, coincidence and fate have long been the domain of storytellers of color, for whom the "naked" force of the world is an everyday experience. In the tradition of African American fiction, for example, coincidence plots and reunion plots are normal. People of color often need coincidence in order to reunite with their kin.

20.

Adoptee stories also frequently feature coincidence and reunion. Maybe that is why I am drawn to external causation, to alternative traditions, to non-Western story shapes. Like Jen, I grew up with fiction that wasn't written for me. My desire to write was probably a desire to give myself the agency I didn't have in life. To give my desires the power of plot.

Cortázar calls plot, that string of causation, an inherent danger to the realistic story. "Reality is multiple and infinite," he writes, and to organize it by cause and effect is to reduce it to a "slice." Plot is always a departure from reality, a symbol of reality. But the power of stories is that we can mistake the symbolic for the real.

21.

In *Maps of the Imagination*, author Peter Turchi writes about invisible conventions such as organizing prose in paragraphs, capitalizing the first letter of a sentence, assuming that the fictional narrator is not the author. These conventions become visible when they are broken. To identify them (these are tools: whose tools are these?) is the first step toward making craft conscious. Craft that pretends it does not exist is the craft of conformity or, worse, complicity.

22.

Here is a convention up for debate, one in the process of becoming visible: in an essay on the pathetic fallacy, author Charles Baxter argues that setting in literary realist fiction should less often reflect the protagonist's inner state. Baxter has seen too much rain when the hero is sad, too many sad barns when the hero has lost a child (as in the famous John Gardner prompt). In reality, rain is not contingent on emotion and objects do not change their appearances to fit people's moods. (The Gardner prompt, to describe a barn from the perspective of a grieving father, is more about what a person in a certain mood would *notice*—but the point holds.) Baxter thinks realism should do more to resist story conventions and accurately represent reality.

Yet on screen, the pathetic fallacy seems widely accepted (especially if there is no voiceover to provide a character's thoughts), and student fiction seems more and more influenced by film expectations than prose expectations.

For a few months, I read almost exclusively fiction by a trio of Japanese writers, Haruki Murakami, Yoko Ogawa, and Banana Yoshimoto. Each seems to offer a world that is very shaped by the interiority of the protagonist. In Murakami's work, it's a fair critique to complain that female characters seem to be who they are because the male protagonists want them to be so. In Yoshimoto's work, characters often seem created solely for their effect on the protagonist: a psychic gives the protagonist a crucial warning, or a dying character shows the protagonist how to live. In Ogawa's work, settings and even mathematical equations represent emotion. There are foils and mirrors and examples of how to act and how not to act and sexual fantasies and supernatural guides and exactly the right wrong partner. In truth, these worlds that seem half the protagonist's imagination give great pleasure. There is a kind of structural pleasure that comes from seeing the pathetic fallacy played out on a grand scale. It's not the pleasure of reality, but of what we sometimes *feel* reality to be, a way of being in the world.

23.

Why, when the protagonist faces the world, does she need to win, lose, or draw? This is a Western idea of conflict. (For more, see the later chapter on redefining conflict.) What if she understands herself as a part of that world,

that world as a part of herself? What if she simply contin-
ues to live?

24.

In *Tiger Writing*, Gish Jen cites a study in which whites and
Asians are asked to identify how many separate events
there are in a specific passage of text. Whites identify more
events, because they see each individual action, such as
"come back upstairs" and "take a shower," which appear
in the same sentence, as separate events—while Asians do
not. Jen writes that the American novel tends to separate
time into events and to see those events as progression, as
development—a phenomenon she calls "episodic specificity." At first, she believed herself to be culturally disadvan-
taged, as a writer, but then she found Kundera and his idea
of the novel as existential rather than a vehicle for plot.

In "Characteristics of Negro Expression," author
Zora Neale Hurston identifies characteristics of African
American storytelling, such as adornment, double descriptions, angularity and asymmetry, and dialect. All
are things often edited out of workshop stories in the
name of craft. Hurston identifies them in order to legiti-
mize them. Craft is in the habit of making and maintain-
ing taboos.

25.

The considerations here are not only aesthetic. To
consider what forces have shaped what we think of as

psychological realism is to consider what forces have shaped what we think of as reality, and to consider what forces have shaped what we think of as pleasurable, as entertaining, as enlightening, in life.

Realism insists on one representation of what is real. Not only through what is narrated on the page, but through the shape that narration takes.

Craft is support for a certain worldview.

If it is true that drafts become more and more conscious, more and more based on decisions and less and less on "intuition," then revision is where we can take heart. Revision is the craft through which a writer is able to say and shape who they are and what kind of world they live in. Revision must also be the revision of craft. To be a writer is to wield and to be wielded by culture. There is no story separate from that. To better understand one's culture and audience is to better understand how to write.

AUDIENCE, THEME, AND PURPOSE

You can't control who reads your fiction, but you can control whom you write for. In 1961, Wayne Booth argued that a work of fiction is always "rhetorical"—that it involves authorial choices that establish an authorial persona (you can't find the real author in the text) and that ask readers to "subordinate" their real beliefs to the beliefs required by the text (e.g. superpowers or space travel). The reader's "second self"—the implied reader—is the one who experiences the characters as people, even if the real self knows that they are made up. The author's "second self"—the implied author—is the version of the author that readers imagine from the text (and even occasionally mistake for the real author).

Let's see the effect in action. Below are two paragraphs set in New York on September 11.

1. From where he stood, the tower seemed to wilt, like a gray flower suddenly losing its petals. It was terrifying, the beauty he could

see in disaster. In the moment, the image was beautiful—indeed, this moment would forever link beauty and tragedy for him, so that later, whenever he saw something beautiful, he would expect the worst to come from it.

2. His phone rang, and he almost dropped it as he answered. It was his mother, calling from Seoul. She had seen some news about New York—wasn't that where he was? He didn't know what he was seeing—it wasn't until later that he knew that two planes had flown into the World Trade Center towers, not on accident but in a planned attack. In the moment, all he could do was reassure his mother that it was a big city, and that he was okay. The line went dead. He tried to call back, but his calls would not connect. That was the problem with America, he thought: it was a country in which you never got the connections you needed.

Forgive my first drafts—the point is this: these two paragraphs evoke two different implied authors and are aimed at two different audiences. The first paragraph assumes that its readers would know more of the context, would likely have seen footage of the towers falling (in order for the simile to work, if it does), and would accept the tragedy as a secondary focus rather than the primary focus (the paragraph is about the effect of that day rather than on its details). The implied author and reader are both Americans old enough to remember that day.

In contrast, the second paragraph assumes the audience needs an explanation, and the prose itself focuses on the confusion not only of the event but of America as a whole. Yet it is also much more in the moment—the moment carries the drama more than its effects. The implied author and reader might be foreign, or younger, without direct experience of 9/11.

The real author—me—is the same. The real reader—you—is the same. You are asked to step into the role of the implied reader, and by figuring out the expectations you should read with, you create an image of the implied author. Craft is about how the words on the page do this: what expectations the writer engages with imply whom both the implied reader and implied author are and what they should believe in and care about, what they need explained and/or named, where they should focus their attention, what meaning to draw from the text.

As writers then, we can think of the implied reader as the perfect reader for our work, who would understand everything and would read the book exactly as we intend. Consider theme. Workshops often discuss theme as if the writer can determine it. But when we put fiction out into the world, readers come up with their own readings of theme. They bring their own experiences and interpretations. The author can determine the theme only for the implied reader—the reader whose experiences and interpretations the author anticipates.

A consideration of theme is always a consideration of audience. A book about a terrible childhood will mean something different for a child than it will for an adult. Which audience are we writing for?

Here's another example a Western reader might be familiar with: Joseph Conrad's novel *Heart of Darkness*. In my PhD program, a famous author echoed a long-held argument that appears to defend Conrad from the charge of racism. Conrad was anti-colonialist, so the racist beliefs in the novel belong only to its narrator, not to him. We can use what we know about the implied reader and implied author to show that the racism is not only in the narrator's perspective, but in Conrad's craft.

Author Chinua Achebe takes this same basic approach in his famous critique of *Heart of Darkness*, "An Image of Africa." Achebe first notes the scarcity of page-time, characterization, and dialogue given to Africans in the novel (craft decisions about what to leave out) as well as the few exceptions to that scarcity (craft decisions about what to include). The three exceptions are Kurtz's mistress and two instances when Africans speak in English— otherwise the narrator describes their speech as a "violent babble of uncouth sounds." Importantly, these exceptions are all used as plot points: to cause a fight, to contribute to the famous "horror," and to affect the narrator's character arc—they have craft purposes. Regarding the idea that this racism is only the narrator's (Marlow's), while Conrad is being ironic and critical, Achebe says:

> Conrad appears to go to considerable pains to set up layers of insulation between himself and the moral universe of his history. He has, for example, a narrator behind a narrator. The primary narrator is Marlow but his account is given to us through the filter of a second, shadowy person. But if Conrad's intention is to draw a cordon sanitaire between himself and the moral and psychological malaise of his narrator his care seems to me totally wasted because he neglects to hint however subtly or tentatively at an alternative frame of reference by which we may judge the actions and opinions of his characters. It would not have been beyond Conrad's power to make that provision if he had thought it necessary.

That is, nothing in the book suggests that the implied reader (and implied author) should not share the narrator's racism. Nothing suggests that the racism is only in the narration and not in the craft. Even when the narrator lets African characters speak and be understood, those possible exceptions to the narrator's racism are used for racist craft purposes—that is, the exceptions are a way for the African characters to be plot tools toward a colonialist plot, rather than a way to offer less colonialist characterization.

If the real Conrad did not intend to be racist, he has made racist choices. His implied reader is not supposed to reject the narrator's racism, but to share in it. As Achebe says, nowhere in the text, even with various levels of narration, is there a hint that the audience should judge Marlow as racist. Conrad isn't able to see the prejudice in his craft: he shares it and expects his audience to share it. Achebe sees the racism because he can't give over his real beliefs to the beliefs in the text. Conrad never, at any point, considered what an actually anti-racist audience would think about the book. A truly anti-colonialist book would have to decolonize its idea of whom it is for.

We need to think about how to make more conscious decisions about audience and what that can do for our fiction. We need to think, in other words, about purpose. (Put theme and audience together, and purpose is what you get.) A book about how terrible childhood is might encourage children to empathize, identify, be afraid, give up, or follow/break the rules, etc. For adults, the purpose might be something more like simple entertainment, or even "Congratulations, you made it," or perhaps: "Look after your children."

For a marginalized writer writing to a normative audience, the writer has to be wary of normative craft. Much of what we learn about craft (about the expectations we are supposed to consider) implies a straight, white, cis, able (etc.) audience. It is easy to forget whom we are writing for if we do not keep it a conscious consideration, and the default is not universal, but privileged. To name the race only of characters of color, for example, because that is how you've seen books do it before, is to write to a white audience. It is to write toward the expectations of how white people read the world. We might think of it as one small concession, but it has real consequences about whom readers must become to read our fiction. And if we start to mix audiences, it quickly becomes difficult to tell what the theme and purpose are at all. To name race for no characters, for example, might seem a tempting solution, but it is a solution for no one except those who know that not naming race is an active choice against naming color. I've gotten into the habit of naming every character's race, since this seems like how race operates when I talk to other people of color. It's a choice about whom my fiction is talking to.

Naming race might be too simple. Let's take a more complicated example, like how to write about microaggressions. Even the term microaggression is loaded and implies a certain audience. I don't teach my Asian American children to tell the difference between microaggressions and macroaggressions; I teach them to recognize racism and what to do about it. The term microaggression is for people who need to distinguish less obvious racist attacks from more obvious racist attacks, or unintentional racism from intentional racism. My struggle is generally with the effects, not with the intention.

When writing about microaggressions, audience is a huge consideration. There is one way of writing about microaggressions that seems aimed at showing that they exist and evoking empathy from people who don't experience them—this is writing microaggressions for a white audience. There is another way of writing about microaggressions that seems aimed at validating other POC experiences—of saying, that thing that happened to you really was racist, you were not imagining it. Then there is a way of writing about microaggressions that is about realism—where microaggressions might not be emphasized, but are included because they are a real part of life. This final way doesn't explain what happened or try to convince anyone. It takes for granted that the audience understands and can fill in all the gaps through shared cultural experience.

These three ways (among others) of writing microaggressions imply three different audiences—and three different themes—and three different purposes. Each has value and can be done well. But let's not forget that it is a craft decision. To demonstrate, let's extend the example to a socially conscious writer of color. If she writes a book about microaggressions to show that they exist and how they affect people of color, the purpose might be to convince the white audience to try to be better allies, but there is no purpose for an audience of color unless it is to convince them to give the book to their white friends/family/coworkers/etc. If the writer writes for an audience of color with the purpose of validation, the audience of color might feel seen while a white audience might not. Feeling seen is valuable, and can but doesn't necessarily encourage social consciousness. Perhaps for a white audience the book requires a leap of faith, for which the reward might be greater empathy. If the writer writes for an audience of color with the inclusion of microaggressions but the purpose, say, to link love to protest—then an audience of color might learn something about love and be inspired to protest, but a white audience might deem the microaggressions extraneous. (We'll look at how white critics attack Chinese fiction in a future chapter.) A certain white reader might not care to read as an outsider, or might be able to jump right in, or might give up. The writer can't determine other people's limitations, only her own.

REDEFINING CRAFT TERMS

Though this list is not meant to be exhaustive, only the beginning of a larger conversation, I have attempted to redefine some often-used craft terms. These redefinitions are meant to be useful in the classroom and/or to the individual writer.

Tone

An orientation toward the world

Let's begin with a term that is rarely defined at all and yet is absolutely foundational. When I was a beginning writer, tone was presented to us mostly as "you know it when you see it." It wasn't often a direct concern in workshop. In fact, the only time I've ever heard it defined by another fiction writer was in an aside, when, in the middle of talking about the middles of novels, Robert Boswell said one could consider tone as *the distance between the narrator and the character.*

This definition was useful to me because it offers a strategy through which a fictional tone can contradict the attitude of its characters—for example, comic novels with serious-minded protagonists. It is easy to see how a narrator who views the seriousness of the characters as funny can produce a comic effect. Another example might be a retrospective narrator who wistfully describes his childhood, though as a child he was not wistful, but curious and eager.

However, *the distance between the narrator and the character* is usually how we define "psychic distance," which is different but related. Psychic distance refers not to any difference of opinion between the narrator and the characters but to how "close" or "far" the narrator gets to a character's mind. In this way, psychic distance is one of many tools a writer can use to create tone—a more distant narrator, for example, might contribute to a more ambiguous tone, or otherwise—as are other tools like the sound or connotation of words, meter, rhythm, etc., even description, setting, characterization, plot (what leads to success or ruin, and the success or ruin itself, often does a lot to establish tone). But none of these things, by itself, is what tone means to a story, what tone *is*.

If we think about what tone *does* for fiction, it seems to offer a kind of lens through which to understand the attitudes of the characters toward each other and toward the world. Deadly serious characters may end up in a novel with a deadly serious tone, and they may also end up in a novel with a comic tone or something else, so our sense of what the tone is helps us figure out how to interpret them. Where does this sense come from? What is it that the author establishes via craft decisions? It is an *orientation toward the world*, the orientation of the implied author.

I steal "orientation" here from the dreaded Aristotle, who describes emotion as an "orientation to the world." By "toward," I want to suggest something less situational, to move from emotion to tone. What Aristotle is saying is that when we feel anger, for example, that anger is a register of our sudden perception of the world: We feel angry because we feel that the world is unjust. A man on the street bumps into you and never apologizes, indicating that he has more of a right to be there than you do. What you register is injustice, and how you register it is anger. In fact, the anger typically arrives before the thought of injustice. The anger is your orientation to an unjust world.

This is why the anger will disappear if the feeling of

injustice disappears (for example, the man stops and offers a sincere apology or he explains convincingly that it
was an accident or he was rushing to save a dog from being
hit by a car). What is important to Aristotle is that *what
you feel* can teach you *what you think.* Emotion is intelligent.

Where we must part from Aristotle is in our current
understanding that emotions are often cultural, not universal or instinctual. (One famous example from anthro-
pology: the emotion "being a wild pig" makes men in New
Guinea steal things and run into the woods, only to remember nothing upon their return. This emotion is socially accepted and normal. It is also learned.)

In other words, an orientation toward the world does
not originate in an individual, but in the world. What we
consider unjust is shaped by shared values. If our culture
says we should be able to own land, then it feels unjust
when a stranger builds his house in our yard. If our culture
says no one owns the land, then it does not feel unjust when
a stranger builds his house in our yard. We have no yard.

The difference between emotion and tone, for our
purposes as writers, is about an overall effect. Tone can
last an entire story. A book that expresses one single, continuous *emotion* would be overwhelming. Emotion shifts
and changes. In a sad tale, the protagonist might feel
angry, happy, optimistic, etc. at various points of time.
(This may be why it is so hard to find a "happy" novel—
happiness is rarely a tone, but often an ending.)

Tone should not be mistaken for the *protagonist's*

orientation toward the world, however, even for a first-person narrator. The protagonist might find the world to be a wonderful place, but the book might contradict her. This kind of contradiction often occurs in satire. The example of the comic novel with the serious narrator works only if it is clear that the book's orientation is different from the protagonist's. Satire works only if it encourages the implied reader to read ironically.

Let's get back to the world, though. Fiction writers typically present a difficult world for their characters (especially if the tone is not ironic). Let's say a writer attempts a *bildungsroman*, a traditional coming-of-age story which, as literary criticism tells us (see the chapter "What Is Craft?"), typically begins with a protagonist on the outside of society and ends with his reincorporation. In this case, say: country boy moves to the city. At first, the city is overwhelming, the people difficult to understand, the boy's dreams seem impossible, maybe someone pickpockets him, etc. The world is not on his side. The tone, however, depends on how the implied reader (see the previous chapter for an explanation of the implied reader) is supposed to see things.

Is it implied/is the implied reader supposed to feel the same as the boy—that the world is indeed too difficult? Is the implied reader supposed to feel the opposite—that it's not the city's problem, it's the boy's? Is the implied reader supposed to find the city repugnant and wish the boy would go back to the country? Is the implied reader supposed to realize that the city is actually the perfect place for the boy? Etc. The implication depends not only on how the author depicts the boy, but on how the author depicts the city, both from within the boy's perspective and (again, see the previous chapter) also outside of it.

If the country boy is to become a city boy, then by the end of this example story: (a) the boy will change so that he fits in; (b) the boy will discover how to love the city for what it is (often mistaken for "learning to love himself"); or (c) the city will change, whether via the boy's actions or an outside force. (At that point the boy can be reincorporated, hooray.)

The tone develops with the characters and the world—here, in the shape of an arc. In a traditional teleological novel, the ending will either decide or fulfill that arc. (This may be one reason why a Western literary audience so easily accepts tonal shifts at the ends of novels and stories.) A comic novel may become tragic if the boy sells himself out to fit in, or it may fulfill the comic if the boy wins the lottery or suddenly discovers a gold mine under his family's ancestral farm.

What tone tells us is that if fiction regularly presents a difficult world, it also indicates how to make sense of that world—and for whom the world is difficult. Whether positive or negative, fiction always says something about how we live, and not in an individual sense but a contextual one. When we write fiction, we write the world. Even if that world looks almost the same as ours, it will always be a representation, not a universal. If there is a distance tone inhabits, it is the distance between our world and the world of the story.

Plot
Acceptance or rejection of consequences

Plot is typically taught as a causal string of events rising out of character. And this concept of plot is useful. It's generally what Western readers expect. It's self-contained. It creates resonance between earlier and later events. Each action a character takes gains suspense and stakes when it is expected to force further actions, to have larger consequences on the character's world. Like each word in a language, each event in a character-driven plot holds meaning because of its place within a chain of connected events, which emphasizes that fiction is more than a set of conversations or happenings, that an individual's choices have and make *meaning*.

Yet it's about time that individual agency stops dominating how we think about plot or even causality. If we canonize E. M. Forster and Aristotle, it should be as representatives of one tradition among many. Aristotle famously put plot first in importance (when writing tragedy) and gave plot a shape and a purpose, and Forster focused plot on causation and character. ("The king died and then the queen died of grief" is a plot, he says, while "The king died and then the queen died" is merely a *story*.) But Aristotle put plot first because he didn't personally like the dominance of theme in drama (and because, as Forster himself points out, drama shows action more easily than it shows thought). Aristotle complains that the tragedians of his day used plot not in service of an individual's tragic agency, but as a way of stringing together various monologues and dialogues by theme. To him, an episodic plot in which a character faces a thematic series of problems rather than bringing those problems upon himself is the worst offense; a real tragedy is the result of a protagonist's one tragic flaw.

Forster's insistence on agency is really about audience. He believes that a series of events that are not causally connected (a war, then an earthquake, then two people falling in love) is for "stupid" readers. An "intelligent" reader's goal is to solve the mystery of causality. It is this mystery that Forster relates to character—what he really means in his famous quote "incident springs out of character" is that the mystery should be human. He is making a claim about the world, that it is a matter of human agency. We may not agree. If I touch a window and it shatters, why should I make sense of this by thinking my touch *caused* the window to shatter? Why shouldn't I think it was a coincidence, and even that the coincidence is what makes it meaningful? Forster and Aristotle object to a coincidental plot for moral reasons that have to do with their belief in the project of the individual.

As a child, I used to read fiction for exactly this sense of agency: to feel that the world, which felt so out of my control, could be controlled. To enter the books of my youth was to enter books in which a world was ordered around an individual. The protagonist walks through a door into a kingdom that has been waiting for just his appearance. Fictional protagonists often have vast incomprehensible power, enough to save worlds, because the worlds are theirs. The plots of these books support the idea that human agency is how to make sense of the human experience. They also support certain ideas about who should have that agency and who should not.

It's no coincidence that most of these books were about well-off white kids. Whom were they written for? Believing that agency is heroic, I felt that my life was villainous. I wanted to change the world, rather than to accept or reject the consequences of living in it. Consequence, in my life, originated in systems of power—whether that meant my family, the adoption industry, the school system, hegemonic normativity, or so on. If we think of plot as *acceptance or rejection of consequences*, we take into account constant negotiations with power. Acceptance and rejection are often emotional, not active. Sometimes a character's negotiations with power are part of a string of causation and sometimes not. To put plot in terms of acceptance and rejection is also to put plot in sociocultural context. Acceptance and rejection are cultural—they depend on positionality, geography, mental health, familial values, trauma, etc.

Causality is an important discussion in fiction, as is agency and separating plot from event. But if the axiom "start when all but the action is finished" is useful, it is possibly because being in the world is much more about dealing with effects than with causes. Fiction in which the world is constantly putting demands on characters, rather than the other way around—like a plague or global warming or fascism—is equally as compelling and true (if not more so to certain audiences). The hero story is its own fantasy. Coincidence, routine, unexplainable emotion, even the weather, can be profound. The king dies, and then the queen dies, but the people still have laundry to do, children to feed, love to love, lives that continue in all directions, not each independent of the other, but more meaningful for how they intersect.

Conflict

What gives or takes away the illusion of free will

When I was a fiction student, I was taught that conflict is what stands in the way of desire. There were two levels (external and internal) and three classes (man vs. man, man vs. world, man vs. self). This definition is an okay start—but it stops before it ever gets to meaning. It implies that conflict can be thrown at a character without consideration of what that conflict signifies.

Of course I did go on to learn about theme and about what conflict means to theme (for example: in a story about the importance of family, a useful conflict might be a friend who wants to take a child away from its family, as opposed to something like a car accident that kills the neighbor's dog). But let's go beyond that to what conflict in a story means about the story's place in the real world.

No fiction exists in a vacuum. Even if a story is just about a character who wants ice cream, the character is not without a context, and neither is the ice cream for that matter, and so neither is the desire or the conflict. A rich able white male character wants ice cream from an ice cream truck passing by his car, as they drive through a Black neighborhood that used to be white before white flight changed its makeup, its economics, its social welfare, etc. In this context, various conflicts might come into play. The author must make a choice, and whatever conflict ends up in the story is exactly that: a *choice*, with consequences and meaning. For example, the author decides to make the protagonist run over a nail, try in vain to flag down help, finally put on his spare tire by himself and follow the sound of the truck to the ice cream. This scenario has conflict, but it means something that the conflict doesn't account for the racial and sociocultural and class contexts, etc. Omission is a crucial craft choice.

In addition, conflict must come *from somewhere*. The kind of conflict in the example above suggests that conflict is about luck/circumstance but can be conquered through free will. That's a moral stance. Fiction is constantly taking moral stances. It's the author's responsibility to *take* responsibility.

One of the major issues I have with the way conflict is currently taught is the idea that it should come out of the protagonist and be solved by the protagonist (see the redefinition of plot). My problem is moral. Straight cis able white male fiction has a tendency to present the world as a matter of free will. The problems are caused by the self and can be solved by the development of the self. And somehow both external and internal conflict is like this.

Take *A Wizard of Earthsea*, by Ursula K. Le Guin, which I taught in an undergraduate novel course (spoilers ahead). I taught the novel because some of my students were eager for genre fiction and because the book is extremely "traditional" in its execution of craft. By this I mean: plot is causal and driven by character, the book moves chronologically but is told from a future point in time, every action and object is deliberate and serves a purpose for the protagonist's arc, etc. (Most fantasy novels are like this.)

In the novel, the main character, Ged, is both the creator of his own major conflict and its solution. Conflict comes in the form a shadow version of him from the world of the dead. Ged releases the shadow when he tries to show off his magical power. When it gets out, it nearly kills him. Scarred and humbled, Ged spends much of the second half of the book fleeing, until he realizes that he must literally face himself. The final boss battle is where Le Guin makes her main departure from the traditional hero's journey. No actual battle occurs; Ged and his shadow simply (in my students' words) "hug it out." Ged recognizes his shadow as a part of himself, and embraces it, becoming whole.

Le Guin has great intentions with this book, not only to take power away from the idea that violent confrontation should provide the solution to conflict, but also to center characters of color. Ged is one of the first protagonists of color in white fantasy. On the other hand, Le Guin avoids the experience of being a person of color. She puts him in a world where his race causes him zero trouble. This is a moral stance. In fact, his main problem is himself, or perhaps a darker version of himself, and his main solution to his problem is himself. This is a moral stance. The novel, intentionally or not, puts forward the idea that everything is up to free will, even for people of color, and that what stands in a person's way is his own darkness.

This isn't Le Guin's intention. Her intention was to upset traditional frameworks. She says so in her afterword. But conflict has consequences for meaning. It's not just something you put in fiction to make a story compelling. Conflict presents a worldview. Simply to choose between man vs. man, man vs. world, or man vs. self is to choose a moral view, to choose a way that the world is presented, to choose an audience, and to choose a message to that audience.

A large part of that message is this: How much of the conflict you face is caused by your own actions? How much is on you? This is a question that has every implication for how to read the contexts of race, class, gender, ability, sexuality, etc. Conflict presents a worldview, along a spectrum from complete agency to a life dictated completely by circumstance. Some lives are *mostly* dictated by circumstance, by fate or DNA or place or other individuals or what have you. Such is not the case for everyone, sure—that's the point. Character should be particular and specific and have a particular and specific context. In that context, the question of how much of the conflict you face is a matter of fate or free will *has meaningful consequences*. Conflict, in context, makes meaning.

Character Arc
How a character changes or fails to change

Story Arc
How the world in which the character lives is changed or
fails to be changed

These arcs work together. I have left the definition of character arc (change or failure to change) the way I learned
it, but story arc was always presented to me as something
more like plot, something like how the character's situation changes or fails to change. (For example, a character
who starts out moral and poor, then becomes immoral
and rich, would have a character arc of moral failure and
a story arc of rags to riches.) It might be more useful to
consider instead how the world is changed or fails to be
changed. The rags-to-riches example can play out in nu-
merous ways—and each way is as much about the world
as it is about the character and her individual situation.
A character who becomes rich by giving up her morality
likely indicates that the world fails to be changed. The
character changes: She accepts the consequences of an
immoral world and adapts by joining in that immorality.
She makes herself appropriate to her world.

Another common rags-to-riches plot is the marriage plot (see: Cinderella). Typically in this case, a poor
straight woman becomes the love object of a rich straight
man and thereby gains wealth. Here the world also fails

to be changed. This world suggests women should become sexual objects to rich men if they want to become rich. Such, of course, is our world, which also has consequences for purpose, theme, and audience. (It should be noted that in many Cinderella stories, the character arc is fairly shallow: the love object starts off being extremely desirable—that is, beautiful, good, selfless, etc.—and her desirability is simply better showcased by a "change" like a makeover. It is her desirability that actually changes the lover, who goes from, say, an asshole-with-a-heart-of-gold to learning how to be a better person.)

As Kurt Vonnegut says (see the chapter "What Is Craft?"), the Cinderella story makes money. People consume it and reproduce it. This means something. There are all sorts of interesting theoretical reasons for this, and most of them boil down to: the story says that there is hope of becoming powerful in a system by accepting your powerlessness within it.

Now take a story like that of a missionary (I know, I know). Say that missionary sets out to change people in a poor, colonized country. Either the mission succeeds or fails—the missionary wins true converts or does not win converts. Let's limit the missionary's arc (assuming she starts as a character believing in missions) to either: fails to change her views on missions or changes her views on missions. What you've got then are basically four possible outcomes. For simplicity's sake:

	Protagonist becomes jaded	Protagonist still loves missions
People are converted	1	2
People are not converted	3	4

Each of these options means something (and means something depending on how it is executed, what exactly the views of the missionary and the potential converts are, etc.). Again, for simplicity's sake, let's just take these four positions at a basic level revolving around the view of missions—just positive or negative (though of course it's a spectrum)—and whether or not the missionary wins converts—just converted or not converted (though this too is a spectrum and brings up the question of what "converted" means). We're also reading teleologically (according to the ending). But:

1. In the first scenario, maybe the missionary does her job "well" and people are converted, but she realizes people were better off before, or that she shouldn't have gotten involved. This story might carry the implication that we need to be cautious about how we use our power, or

something like this, because the system is powerful and people can abuse that power.

2. In the second scenario, the story is religious and says that missions are clearly good things. Unless we are supposed to see around the character and come to the conclusion that her actions are not supportable.

3. In the third scenario, maybe the missionary isn't able to convert anyone and learns a lesson about what kind of role she plays, about her own assumptions re: what is moral or charitable being complex and problematic. This story might say something about how missions are colonialist and shouldn't happen. Or it might say that the world is not as vulnerable to conversion as some might think.

4. In the fourth scenario, the story might be telling missionaries to keep trying, that missions are not always successful. Or we might be encouraged to see around the character and even condemn her—which could carry the meaning that we, for example, should see how we are complicit in systems of power.

Of course these are only possibilities, but the point is that the story arc is always read together with the character arc to create meaning. Readers constantly read the two off of each other, whether they realize it or not. And the writer is better off if she is aware of the ways in which she participates in and creates meaning—so that she can mean things more consciously and conscientiously.

To close, I'll give an example of a film I saw with my daughter, then six, a film that fails to account for the implications of story arc on meaning. The film is *Curious George*. In the climactic series of scenes leading to the ending, George and the man with the yellow hat race through the city with a holographic projector, hoping to save a museum by duping people into thinking they see a real artifact. George activates the projector and his giant image causes massive destruction in the city. In the end, the man has to tell everyone he doesn't have what was promised. As he mopes about this, he lets George get captured by animal control and causes three accidents. Finally his girlfriend gives him a pep talk, and he illegally boards the ship taking George back to the jungle. In the jungle, they find the real artifact, and they return to New York as heroes.

The man in the yellow hat undergoes a character change: he learns to value his monkey-friend more than physical successes, and by doing so saves the museum. This is supposed to be a triumphant ending. Yet the story arc, if we ask how the world is changed, is that the man and the monkey cause mass destruction in their attempt to hoodwink people, plus they move an artifact from a colonized country to a colonizer country.

What is the meaning then of the film? Perhaps that doesn't matter much to some people, but it matters to me. I took a child to watch something I hoped she would enjoy, to bond a little, to have some escape from our grief after my wife died. And my daughter did enjoy it, but I was left to consider what it was teaching her about white male privilege, the privilege to destroy a city and face no criminal charges, only celebration. That is the story arc, these are the facts. Whether she knows it or not, my daughter has consumed a cultural message.

Characterization

What makes one character different from everyone else

One of my favorite exercises for characterization I learned from a quick craft class led by the author Danzy Senna: Start a series of sentences about the same character with "S/he/they were the kind of person who . . ." One of the best things about this exercise is that as you exhaust what you already know (both personally and culturally) about what kind of character the character is, you get to really interesting discoveries about what makes your character a "kind."

I also like what Margot Livesey used to teach us—to think about a character's "attitude"—and I have taught attitude alongside Janet Burroway's four methods of direct characterization: "speech, action, appearance, and thought," focusing especially on action and decision, which seem perennial oversights. To that end, an exercise that has helped my students and myself with characterization, plot, world-building, and so forth, is to write a list of every decision a character makes in a story, in order, skipping nothing, not even what they choose to wear that day or negative choices (things they choose *not* to do).

But really what makes a character the kind of person they are is: difference in relation to others, whether that is difference in type or difference in attitude. Just as any story begins with something out of the ordinary (a journey, a visit from a stranger), any character begins in differentiation. In other words, there is no "everyman" character; there is only the character who seems most culturally normal (to a given audience) when compared to the rest of the cast.

What I like about defining characterization via difference is:

1. It makes it obvious when a character's one difference from other characters is her race or sexuality or ableness or class (etc.). Too often these identity markers are the only form of characterization, for supporting characters in particular, which means that the author thinks, for example, being Asian *is* characterizing in a way that being white is not, and therefore has not thought beyond Asianness to what makes a character stand apart.

2. It acknowledges the usefulness of "types" to differentiate, especially when the character is the only one of that type in a story. Take, for example, the charismatic asshole with a heart of gold who learns through love to take care of others (many K-dramas). This is a type, of course, but the type provides a character who: (a) changes over the course of the story and (b) both fulfills and surprises the audience's expectations (often simultaneously). This character is usually the protagonist and is

different from the other characters around him. The same is true of the wealthy man who sees through the posturing of his other wealthy friends, yet can't bring himself to give up that world (Newland Archer in *The Age of Innocence* or most love interests in a Jane Austen novel).

3. Writing other characters with similar but different types in fact helps make each type stand out. One of the best ways to emphasize the heart of gold the asshole has is to introduce an asshole without a heart of gold (and/or the "too nice" character who gets stuck in the friend zone). The easiest way to invite sympathy for a character is to write in a worse character. The easiest way to make the protagonist's change stand out is to write a similar character who is never able to change. Characters (fictional beings that require meaningful choices) always exist in relation to each other (and the world). They may be opposite (foils) or similar except for some crucial difference (mirrors) or models of different ways of becoming (often mothers and fathers) or so on. But like a single word in a system of language, what gives a character meaning is its difference from others.

4. This definition takes the focus off the

dreaded "relatability" argument (that what makes a character compelling has to do with similarities between the character and readers). As an example, take the novel *Blindness*, by José Saramago, in which a virus makes everyone blind except for one woman. Some readers may be tempted to see themselves in this character—but this identification is not the effect of both reader and character being able to see, it's the effect of having only one character who can see. She is compelling not because of any likeness, but because everyone else is the same.

5. Let's come back to language. Contemporary theory tells us that the word "leg" would mean nothing without the words "body" and "arm" and etc. In the same way, characters in a piece of fiction carry and convey meaning within their specific context (of other characters and of world and of other fictional elements like plot or theme). Take Newland Archer out of high society New York and put him in a group of gamblers in Las Vegas, and the meaning of his character and his arc becomes vastly different. Make the novel about how great it is to be part of a group rather than the danger to individual desire, and the meaning of his character and his arc becomes vastly different.

6. It helps with writing genre as much as with writing literary fiction—there's no barrier to entry. It's easy to explain that what makes an elf an elf may be his difference from a human or an orc (different types), but what makes an elf a Legolas is his difference from other elves (difference within the same type).

Relatability
How the characters are presented to the implied reader

Relatability, as it is usually spoken of, is useless to craft. When we say a character is "relatable," what we typically mean is that we are able to invest the character with our own experiences. Bringing one's own experience to the page, however, is always a part of reading—it's unavoidable and has nothing to do with the author's choices (craft). I have argued here for a definition of craft that indeed rests on this very fact: that readers' expectations for fiction are created by their previous experiences with fiction—in other words, by culture. When writers use craft, they are making choices based on which cultural expectations to engage with. A film can use a shot of a keyhole to invest a scene with the tension of other scenes with shots of a keyhole—the shot will carry tension if viewers have watched enough movies to know that it implies that someone or something dangerous is on the other side (regardless of whether or not anything ends up being there in a particular case).

When most readers say they find a character "relatable" then, either (a) they are talking not about the choices of the author but about themselves, or (b) they are obscuring the usefulness of a discussion about who the intended audience is and how the author works with that specific audience's expectations in mind.

Here's an example: an extraterrestrial main character

has its heart broken, so it drinks some alcohol, takes a sleeping pill, watches TV, cries, eats a tub of ice cream, and goes to sleep on a bed.

The interesting thing here is not how relatable the extraterrestrial is—if there is interest in the similarities to white middle-class American grieving habits, then the interest lies in the disconnect between those habits and a space alien. That disconnect in fact encourages readers to make a connection thematically: Perhaps the story is about what it takes to be white, middle-class, and American, or the story asks us to look at how our lives have become alien to us. Etc.

If the alien were to grieve in a way completely outside of human experience, then the comment "How relatable!" would be replaced with the comment "How imaginative!" If, instead of a space alien, the character were an alien from a non-Western country performing non-Western grief, then the comment from a Western audience will often become (whether direct or implied): "How exotic!"

In fifteen years of workshop, I have heard many comments that amount to "How *un*relatable!" but none has been anything other than an attempt to *avoid* talking about craft. To say a work of fiction is unrelatable is to say, "I am not the implied audience, so I refuse to engage with the choices the author has made."

If relatability were somehow a goal of craft, then the question should be: How can a writer go about trying to make a piece of fiction relatable? If we mean "relatable"

as sharing a reader's experience, the first place to go is
audience. We must always ask: Relatable *to whom*? Which
brings us back to the elephant in the room—to call a manuscript "relatable" is really to make a claim about who the
audience is or should be.

Should the author revise her manuscript to make it
more relatable to the reader at hand (i.e. the workshop)?
This takes us into dangerous territory. A writer can easily
lose her way by trading her audience for someone else's.

Instead, let us be specific. Say we give the protagonist
a knitting hobby. This might make her more relatable to
some readers, but the real work is in its specificity. Even
better, the protagonist knits tiny sweaters for her pet sal-
amanders, all named Sally—this would do more to characterize her but likely would make her less "relatable" as
the term is typically used.

Since the act of reading *always* involves bringing one's
experience to a text, a specific reader may for her own reasons relate to a dragon character more than to a human
knitter—the usefulness of relatability to craft is really
about how an implied author presents a character to an
implied reader (see the chapter "Audience, Theme, and
Purpose" for an explanation of implied author and implied reader). To continue the dragon example: if you look
at a dragon one way, it's evil, and if you look at it another
way, it's good. (If you look at Robin Hood one way, he's a
thief, and if you look at him another way, he's a hero.) In
fiction, the author decides *how we look*—or how the implied

reader looks—which means the author decides whether a
character is (implicitly) "relatable" or not, and for whom.

Take for another example, one written and relatively
well-known, the white grandmother in the story "A Good
Man Is Hard to Find," by Flannery O'Connor. In the
story, the grandmother wants to vacation in Tennessee,
not Florida, where her family wants to go. On the trip,
she hides her cat in the car; tells a story about a Black boy
who eats a watermelon, using racist terms; and lies about
a secret door to excite her grandkids, hoping to convince
her son to go where she wants. Via tone, references to re-
ligion, relations to other characters, the grandmother's
manipulations, etc., readers typically get the impression
that they should disapprove of the grandmother. This
impression is an impression of how they should read. In
other words: how the implied reader reads. The change
in the story (O'Connor calls it "grace") comes at the end,
when the grandmother is about to die and recognizes her
murderer as her "son" (as one of the same Christian flock).
The "grace" here relies on readers interpreting the grandmother one way earlier and a new way at the moment of
her death. (The reader who cheers the grandmother on
the entire story will not interpret the ending as a sudden
change for the good but as something else entirely.) The
ability of the real reader to share the implied reader's beliefs gives a story its maximum (intended) impact. (As I've
grown older, for example, I have found the story less personally compelling than I first did when I was eighteen

and regularly attended mass.) The craft is in implying a reader meant to dislike the grandmother, not in whatever arbitrary experiences and opinions the real reader brings to the text.

As a final example, let's go back to the white middle-class American extraterrestrial. Again, the author who addresses relatability as a craft issue has some choices to make about who her implied reader is and how she should present her characters to her chosen audience. If the implied reader is a white middle-class American who lives a life much like the extraterrestrial's, then it makes a huge difference whether or not that reader is supposed to find the alien sympathetic, heroic, disgusting, humorous, tragic, etc. If the implied reader is meant to feel disgust toward the alien, then she is meant to question what that disgust says about herself, when the only thing "unrelatable" about the alien is that it is an alien. In other words, the author may choose to leave the steps of the grieving process exactly the same no matter what version of the story (with what implied reader) ever gets published— what changes in the story isn't the relatability of the experience; what changes is something that could usefully be called "relatability."

Believability

The differences and similarities between various characters' expectations

One of the most distracting conversations in workshop occurs in the name of "believability." "It's not believable," one reader says about an all-day bike ride (to use an example from my MFA); "it's not realistic, this wouldn't happen." It's obvious, though, that this criticism can't be literal, since the same person might happily read about wizards or watch a superhero film.

In the actual workshop in which this bike-ride complaint gobbled up five minutes of a half-hour critique, the writer used his chance to speak at the end of workshop to say: "I did this bike ride. I'm the character."

Neither the criticism nor its defense were helpful in a craft sense.

A popular workaround comes in the form of: "It breaks the rules of the story." This teaches writers to build into earlier parts of the story the possibility for the story to do something "unbelievable" or "unrealistic" later. It's not a bad solution—this is certainly one way of making something strange seem less strange—but it doesn't actually get at the operative element. It is a solution that says: make the strange less strange. It works for the kind of magical realism where no one thinks magic is out of the ordinary, but not for the kind of story where the surprise of a new element is *supposed* to shift the story to new ground.

Take, for example, a domestic drama about a couple falling apart. They fight, they break up. They go their separate ways. One of them falls ill and dies. The other goes to the wake, to remember their good times. At the wake the body stands up and starts eating brains. Now it's a zombie story.

You could build the possibility of zombies into the rules of the story, the way "A Good Man Is Hard to Find" starts with the grandmother not wanting to go to Florida where the criminal called the Misfit has broken out of prison, and ends with the Misfit killing the grandmother—you could make the illness mysterious or give one of the lovers a dream about zombies or set their first date at a zombie flick—but it's not necessary that you *should* plant these kinds of seeds.

It's not actually prior rules that make zombies seem like a frustrating turn of events or an interesting one. Some of it is personal taste or the question of audience—I never questioned the bike ride in my MFA workshop because I didn't care whether a bike ride could go on all day or not; I would be happy to see zombies interrupt a familiar domestic story. On a craft level, the complaint that something is not "believable" or "realistic" or that we don't "buy it" or that it's not "earned" is really an indication that the story doesn't seem to recognize that something unusual has happened. This is why planting seeds is one way to make the change read more "smoothly." But it's not the only way.

One of the most useful tricks I learned in my MFA

was Margot Livesey's response to a believability complaint: "Just make someone in the story question it." If a character within the story brings up the objection, then readers are often happy to let someone else make it. This also gives the writer a chance, whether she uses it or not, to provide context.

This may be why it is so common for novel characters to say they feel like they are in a novel, and why it is so common for movie characters to say they feel like they are in a movie. It is like preemptively addressing the opposing viewpoint in a debate.

Where something like a craft of believability could be useful to the fiction writer is in the difference between multiple characters' reactions. In the kind of magical realism where magic is normal, no characters question the magic. They all expect it. If one character, for example, questions the dead lover becoming a zombie, but everyone else sees it coming, this is a different story than if everyone sees it coming or no one sees it coming or half and half.

Really the shock from the sudden appearance of a zombie is not unlike the shock from reading that a person has ridden a bike all day without stopping or, for that matter, that zombies which started out slow and stumbling have suddenly become fast and athletic. The change might be most useful if it is addressed. An unusual event does the most work for a story when it involves the development of belief or disbelief—once I heard Kazuo Ishiguro talk about strangeness as a dial, that he thinks of it as turning the dial up or down, that if a tiger walks into a board-room and everyone freaks out, the dial is turned down to our "reality," and if everyone ignores the tiger, the dial is turned far up. A tiger walking into a boardroom can tell you what kind of story you're in, but/and it can also *change* what kind of story you're in. I'm a sucker for when a story can pull off the change, when it can break its own rules or suddenly make completely different rules make sense.

I find that the question of who believes something happened or not comes up a lot in life. It usually has to do with privilege. Again, microaggressions can serve as a useful example. It's not unusual, in my experience, that to speak about a microaggression to a white audience is to have it or its racism called into question. This happens in workshop as it happens on the internet. I have been in multiple workshops where white students have basically said either *No one is that bad* or *That isn't so bad.* Then there's the comment that starts with "not all" and ends with embarrassment. I've had peers tell me I need to in-clude non-racist white people "for balance."

These are foremost questions of audience, since in workshop believability is usually leveled against events and characteristics that most of the workshop has not ex-perienced or has the privilege to ignore. And the writer can choose not to address such an audience. The point is that believability can be utilized, rather than simply ad-dressed or avoided, if it is redirected away from who is doing the believing *of* the story toward who is doing the believing *within* the story. Beliefs sometimes seem like the last things writers give characters, far lower on the list than facial features or fashion sense (yes, this is about expectations). Yet the measure of belief within a story is something an author can actually control and use to say something about the world of the story and even about the world in which we live.

Vulnerability

The real author's stakes in the implied author

I often use the first week of workshop to discuss vulnerability with my students, as it is essential to both committed writing and committed workshopping. However, it can be difficult to explain how a writer's vulnerability gets into a story, especially one that does not use the facts of the writer's life, only her imagination. To further complicate things, the book world often demands vulnerability disproportionately from writers of color, especially from women of color and LGBTQ+ people of color—as if these writers are expected to put their lived experience on display in order to publish. This demand for personal vulnerability starts with our cultural expectation that people of color should submit themselves for public consumption (consumption that is economic, intellectual, and emotional). In other words: like everything else, vulnerability is a matter of privilege and power and must be considered within a system of privilege and power.

Vulnerability in fiction is often spoken of as if it is transactional—the author's vulnerability for the reader's—but in fact it starts long before a writer reaches an audience. The obvious example is the diary, in which the owner risks vulnerability because she doesn't expect to be read at all. This kind of vulnerability can make diaries very compelling. As soon as the diary *is* read, the writer does become vulnerable in a certain way, but a different kind of vulnerability exists from the first word. This is the vulnerability between the writer and the persona of the writer that her language creates.

This "created" persona formed by the real writer's craft choices and by the way those choices are read and create meaning—is earlier in this book referred to as the "implied author." (See the chapter "Audience, Theme, and Purpose.") The implied author is not the same as the real author since the implied author exists only in the text. Nor is the implied author the same as the narrator—for example, imagine a satire in which the narrator hates nature and tries to destroy it, but the implied author takes a friendlier stance, which is partly how we understand that we should read the narrator satirically. The real author does not need to include her trauma in the name of vulnerability. Vulnerability is more about the investment an author makes in creating a persona that is adequate to the challenges of the text—and its audience.

In other words, if in the example of the nature satire above, the real author doesn't care about nature one way or the other, it will be difficult to invest the implied author with a satirical view of its nature-hating narrator. If the real author hates nature, it may be difficult to satirize the narrator at all unless there is some real investment in the implied author's nature-love. The real risk in "A Good Man Is Hard to Find," for instance, is not in the sympathy the story shows its murderer (whom O'Connor, in real life, called a prophet), but in the disdain the implied author establishes for the grandmother despite O'Connor's plan to offer the character grace.

We risk something in each creation simply by creating a version of ourselves on the page. That risk is not for sale, but it is on display. If we care to write to a real audience, we should care what our persona implies about us in real life. The writer who claims the freedom to write from any perspective, say, should be aware that it takes an investment in that perspective on the page, and that this investment is open to critique in the real world. If we don't invest in our implied author, why should anyone else? The worst fiction we can write is fiction that doesn't even speak for itself.

Setting
Awareness of the world

It has somehow become common to praise setting for being "a character" of its own, but let's face it: setting is not character. The settings most typically said to be characters are settings that are underrepresented in the dominant fiction tradition. *Setting as character* is often a veiled way of praising work from or, even more so, *about* minority communities, if that work is considered evocative by a white audience.

This is because setting is about what is *noticed*. Sometimes, as in a human narrator visiting an alien planet for the first time, what is noticed might also sync up with what the audience is curious about—how different this planet is from Earth. But in other cases, as in an alien narrator returning to its planet, what is noticed might be quite different from what the audience is curious about—this alien might be more interested in how different its home is now from the last time it lived there. If the alien focused instead on how different its planet is from Earth, then it must be presumed that it is telling its story *for humans*—which, of course, is fine here since the author and audience are not alien. Where things get more complicated is if, for example, instead of a story about an alien, you have a story about an immigrant returning to the nation she left, written by an immigrant author for an immigrant audience. Or even a farm kid returning to the farm for an audience of current and former farm kids (if this farm story explains what a tractor is, it rejects its readers' place in its world, catering instead to an outside gaze). When I was a kid, I liked school stories in which smart outsiders earned their classmates' respect by solving some difficult problem. Yet these books often tricked me into thinking that I could do the same, when my intelligence only encouraged racial discrimination ("you're only smart because you're Asian"). The schools in these novels were, in many ways, similar to my school, but what was noticed was vastly different. This is about setting. I seemed to live in an entirely different world. The effect was to tell me that my kind of outsider would never be accepted.

If I've gotten away from how to *use* setting, it's because the effects of noticing are profound. What is noticed depends on who does the noticing. Cold weather affects someone not used to cold weather far more than it affects someone who is used to it. A strange man in an otherwise empty parking lot is a different setting for a female protagonist than for a male protagonist. A speed trap is a different setting for a Black protagonist than for a white protagonist. A staircase is a different setting for a protagonist in a wheelchair than for a protagonist who can easily ascend it. Etc. Perhaps one of the reasons a white author might have trouble writing a protagonist of color is that the author is noticing the wrong things. The author is thinking of setting as a character of its own rather than reliant on character.

Like everything else, setting is tied intrinsically to character, plot, theme, arc, and so on. A narrator who doesn't notice the economy collapsing is different and has a different arc that says something different about the world than a narrator who notices nothing but the economy collapsing or than a narrator who notices the economy collapsing but really has to figure out how to take care of an ailing family member or escape a murderous ex or so forth. Ask yourself some of these questions:

- What is your protagonist aware of?
- What forces shape her/his/their awareness?
- What is the narrator aware of?
- What forces shape that awareness?
- What awareness shapes the idea of who the implied author is?
- What awareness shapes the idea of who the implied reader is?

What is noticed says something about what is worth noticing and who is worth noticing and what world the characters—and author and audience—accordingly inhabit.

Pacing
Modulation of breath

When I first started writing, pacing seemed to be a matter of math. Chapters were supposed to be ten to twenty pages long. Workshop stories were supposed to be ten to twenty pages long. I heard that a famous professor at Iowa taught a course in which all stories had to be exactly fifteen pages, which he said was the perfect length for publication. I read, in a craft book by a literary writer who turned to genre, that all chapters should be *under* ten pages. A professor in my PhD program mentioned that one way to keep up the pace of a novel is to cut the chapters in the middle of an arc rather than at the end of an arc. He said this about a book he hadn't liked but nonetheless had read at a quick pace, unable—as they say—to put it down, because he didn't want to leave off in the middle of a chapter.

When I planned my first novel, which became my second novel, I planned twenty chapters, each about fifteen pages in length, each from a different perspective, with an intermission in the exact center, after chapter ten. There was other math too, but (like all math) I've forgotten it. After a few years of writing this novel—tearing it apart and putting it back together again, combining two characters into one protagonist, moving the entire story back in time by three years, and writing in a massive flood—the math became harder and harder to achieve. How to keep my chapters to similar lengths when the flood was such a huge (and lengthy) part of the book, and when some characters needed more room than others? I felt forced to make choices that were at best arbitrary.

On the other hand, workshop had taught me to write stories ten to twenty pages long, since shorter stories didn't seem to provide enough to talk about, which meant workshop would digress or resort to asking for more of so and so or such and such (the easiest and laziest comment is *Tell me more about X*), and longer stories seemed to annoy my peers. This made me used to a certain pace, where a story had to start, expand, and come to some kind of ending in more than three thousand and fewer than five thousand words.

The *Merriam-Webster* definition of "modulate" includes the idea of "tuning" to a key or pitch, or keeping in measure or proportion, as well as the idea of "varying" amplitude, frequency, or phase "for the transmission of information." To modulate breath, then, is both to be in tune to one's breath and to vary it. I was doing the opposite: fighting myself and trying to stay consistent.

After about half a decade of revision, I finally got up the courage to throw out the idea of chapters altogether. It felt terrifying and wrong, but by getting rid of my expectations of what a chapter is supposed to be, I was able to find a pace that fit both my pitch and the information I was trying to transmit. I see my students make the same mistake now. Even after I warn them about my own experience, they might write a fight scene the same length as a memory the same length as a revelation and so forth. We can find our drafts out of proportion if we don't think of each section as in proportion to difference.

And so we come back to difference again. Difference not only between chapters and scenes and paragraphs and sentences, but also between characters, and perspectives, and so forth. To play two different perspectives in the same key is not to play in tune to either. Breath also differs for each author—some write long, and others struggle to ever write a scene of more than three pages. Some authors have been taught to speak quickly if they want to get a word in; others have been taught to hold forth. Breath, too, is about power: it is gendered, raced, etc. To modulate breath means to think about the frequencies we've been taught to speak on, and to tune in to how we transmit information and what kind and to whom. To modulate breath means more awareness of when we speed up or slow down or pause, the variations within our breath and between breaths, and the effect of sharing breath with a reader—what demands a story might make on breath, how a story might teach its audience to match its rhythm, how certain genres and/or readers prefer certain keys or measures, or what happens when a story suddenly shifts key, like a bridge in a pop song—etc. I prefer this way of talking about tuning in to ourselves and our audience to sayings like "finding your voice"—which seems more about the cultural constructions that make us say one person has a "voice" and another does not and what kind of voice is acceptable, unique, bold, etc.—or to terms like "quiet" or "demanding" or "hooks you from the very first page," which are often more about our expectations of who should be quiet and who demands our attention.

Structure

The organization of meaning

A word gets its meaning from a system of other words. The pronoun "he" on its own refers to no one and has no meaning; the word "fish" in the sentence "We were playing *Go Fish*" has a different meaning than in the sentence "We caught a fish." A fish is the kind of animal that swims in the sea and lays eggs only because we have other words for other kinds of animals, such as "mammal" and "bird."

Similarly the word "fish" can take on a particular meaning within the system of a particular story, for example if the last time a boy saw his mother was on a fishing trip, or if the mother, say, turned into a fish. Any part of any story has its particular meaning only within the system of that story (as any story has meaning only within a system of other stories—a culture).

Meaning is also affected by placement—the word "fish" takes on its particular story meaning only after we know that the mother is now a fish. Before we know this, we may be searching for the meaning of fish or we may assume the meaning that our personal and cultural context makes us most familiar with. A reader who hates fish, for example, may take her hatred into the story. A reader who loves fish may take her love into the story. Almost nothing in a story is neutral, since almost everything in a story contributes to the context in which the story's audience finds meaning.

This is true even in the order of two sentences, as in "Kim was afraid of apples" and "Kim ate an apple." If Kim eats the apple before her fear, it is possible to read these sentences as meaning that eating the apple made Kim afraid of apples. If Kim eats the apple after her fear, then it is possible to read these sentences as meaning that Kim overcame her fear of apples. (Of course, you can also change the order of individual words: "An apple ate Kim." This may be a good reason to fear apples.)

This example may also be complicated through how much space comes between the sentences. A story that starts with "Kim was afraid of apples" and ends with "Kim ate an apple" would likely encourage its reader to interpret what comes between as what helped Kim overcome her fear. The eating of an apple would signal a much greater meaning. On the other hand, a story that has the two sentences somewhere in the middle, with one sentence in between (say: "Kim was afraid of apples. Yoon ate an apple. Kim ate an apple.") would also give meaning to the act of eating the apple, but that act might not be interpreted as a major change, rather as a response, an attitude, an attraction, etc.

The above assumes that things are chronological, but even when the sentences do not follow chronology, placement matters. "Kim ate an apple. In the past, Kim had been afraid of apples." This order is still different from: "In the past, Kim had been afraid of apples. Kim ate an apple." The difference may be slight, but there is a difference. Consider this: "In the past, Kim had been a racist. Kim hugged her Asian friend." Versus: "Kim hugged her Asian friend. In the past, Kim had been a racist." One comes as a revelation.

Extended to larger parts of a story, like scene, the order of things is crucial. Take a story like Jhumpa Lahiri's "Hell-Heaven," in which a daughter narrates her mother's crush on a family friend. At the end of the story, the grown-up narrator reveals a secret: that after the friend got married, the mother doused herself in gasoline and stood in the yard with matches. The final line of the story is about how the narrator came to know this secret. It gives us the context of this revelation: the mother revealed her near-suicide when the narrator's own heart was broken. We are reminded that amid the drama of her mother's unrequited love, the daughter not only played witness but also lived her own life affected by the love she witnessed. Before this ending, it is easy to forget about the narrator as an active character, since the mother's story is so compelling. The secret reconfigures meaning. To reveal it at the beginning would have made it a lens rather than a shared act relegating the daughter to the background of her own childhood.

When I first wrote this definition, one of my classes had just workshopped a story about a brown woman whose brother is a drug dealer and a white cop who shows up in the neighborhood wanting to do good. This is a story that could easily go wrong, but the student author organized it so that it starts and ends with the brown character's perspective. The white cop intrudes in the middle. A story that used the same events but started and ended with the policewoman would convey a very different meaning simply because of its structure.

In Manuel Gonzales's story "Farewell, Africa," which takes place in a near future in which the water level rises and submerges certain parts of the world, the narrator is a reporter who attends a kind of Met Gala full of privileged guests. The central work of art is supposed to be a reenactment of the continent of Africa sinking into the ocean while a famous speechwriter reads the famous speech he once wrote for the actual tragedy. The conflict in this story is that the mechanics of the art installation won't work—in the middle of the gala, Africa *isn't* sinking. Gonzales gives us a story about, among other things, privilege and global warming. The story is broken into five sections, the first centered around the artist, the second around the museum curator, the third around the speechwriter, the fourth around the reporter, and the last around the absurd piece of art in the center of all this. In other words, the reporter-narrator chooses to privilege the first four perspectives over the horrific real event that has become an imaginary problem for the gala. The story ends with the speechwriter saying, "They told us the center will not hold . . . yet here we are." "We" here refers to the privileged attendees, and the center refers to an Africa that was swallowed by the sea. Through structure, Gonzales is able to make the absurdity and satire clear—the organization of these five parts shows the attention paid to the "we" while the real tragedy comes last.

It is important to consider how the order of things affects the importance given to them. But I will close with a note on how the importance given to ordering is cultural. Americans often seem obsessed with what comes first—with beginnings, with "newness" or "originality"—and with what comes last—with what is dominant in the end. Most Americans are taught in school and through the books they read and by American history and imperialism to interpret stories teleologically. Teleology, it can also be argued (and this argument has been made very persuasively, especially by women writers), is gendered—as mentioned earlier in the book, Jane Alison calls the conventional importance of the ending a "bit masculosexual." The evaluation of meaning by how things end appeals to a sense of domination, as in the story of colonization. In some cultures, there are no lasts, only cycles, and firsts are politely refused or mistrusted. As always, structure organizes meaning in a certain way only directed toward a certain audience, and the author's choice of audience, whether intentional or not, is the foundational choice.

AN EXAMPLE FROM EAST ASIAN AND ASIAN AMERICAN LITERATURE

In his book on creative writing programs during the Cold War, *Workshops of Empire*, Eric Bennett traces the success of the workshop model to its history at the Iowa Writers' Workshop. He quotes letters from Workshop cofounder Paul Engle to friends and funders, in which Engle sometimes describes his investment in craft as an ideological weapon against the spread of Communism. In one letter, Engle writes that he is convinced, "with a fervor approaching smugness," that the tradition of Western literature "is precisely what these people [in the East], in their cloudy minds, need most."

As proof that the Workshop's values were indeed spreading, one of the very first immigrant writers Engle championed was a Korean, Kim Eun Kook, who soon after graduation published a bestselling novel under the name Richard Kim. The novel, *The Martyred*, is about a Korean reverend falsely accused of betraying his fellow

Christians in the name of Communism. Bennett writes that Kim was known in the Workshop as the Korean vet who "took so long to read an English sentence that no one could remember what was wrong with it" and who kept asking the "annoying" question "But what is the *meaning* of that?" (Bennett's emphasis).

It makes sense that someone learning new cultural rules of craft would want to know the significance of a character-driven plot, and limiting the use of adjectives, and showing vs. telling, etc. So what was so annoying about the question? To admit that craft has meaning is to admit that it is not a default, that it means *something* to *someone*.

If you have been taught to write fiction in America, it is a good bet that you have been taught a style popularized by Ernest Hemingway and later by Raymond Carver, sometimes described as "invisible," that is committed to limiting the use of modifiers and metaphors, to the concrete over the abstract, to individual agency and action, and to avoiding overt politics (other than the politics of white masculinity). Instead of a political argument, a character might angrily eat a potato. This is supposed to leave conclusions up to readers, though what it really means is that the ideology of craft is to hide its ideology. Bennett, like Kim, wants to know, what is the *meaning* of that? Why did this craft model that emphasizes restrained formal techniques become so dominant? The answer Bennett comes to is that limits and formal concerns are easy to regulate and reproduce. If the Workshop is supposed to spread American values without looking like it is spreading American values, what better craft for the job than the craft of hiding meaning behind style?

There is an international complaint that Americans rarely read in translation and that their fictional landscapes are comparatively insular. It's a complaint that I dislike, because it stereotypes and because it equates "American" with white and/or English-native, but a typical school reading list does suggest that most Americans are far more versed in a single *tradition* of fiction than in any other. If we read a few translations or foreign classics, they are often compared to the tradition of Western psychological realism (in it or not in it) rather than read within traditions of their own.

There is no universal standard of craft—this can't be emphasized enough—but this in no way means that fiction can be separated into on the one hand Western realism and on the other hand various exceptions to it (*genre* or *foreign* or *experimental* or so on). Instead, we must view other standards as exactly that—not as exceptions but as norms.

Diversity, in the parlance of our times, should not be tokenism. I have been guilty as a teacher of trying to represent in one course as many different books as possible. But then students tend to fall back on reading these books *against* the main tradition they have already been taught. Craft is not about cultural exceptions, but about cultural expectations—which means we need to understand traditions, not individual books. We need to learn both the conventions of a tradition and the experiments and exceptions and other genres that have influenced, resisted, and changed it. The tradition of stories within stories, looping or intersection or nesting or framing or so forth, in which we could include contemporary novels like the American middle-grade novel *Where the Mountain Meets the Moon*, by Grace Lin, and the Chinese literary novel *Life and Death Are Wearing Me Out*, by Mo Yan, is a tradition that goes back at least to the *Thousand and One Nights*. A better understanding of this tradition would, for example, have allowed critics to see recent novels like Kate Atkinson's *Life After Life* or David Mitchell's *Cloud Atlas* as Western adaptations of long-held Eastern storytelling practices rather than as products of brilliant innovation. How can a writer know the many possibilities of what they *can* do without knowing many different ways that things have been done before and where their possibilities have come from?

Because craft is about expectations, unfamiliarity is one of craft's most serious problems. In workshops, this unfamiliarity is often truly dangerous for the writer who *is* familiar with and/or may be working in other traditions. The workshop may read her work within a tradition to which she does not belong—and the workshop is persuasive and powerful. To break the rules as an experiment is one thing, but to want to write toward other rules that better represent one's reality (for example) is another. The American writer of color who wants to break free of the white literary tradition might unsurprisingly think her only option is experimentalism. To experiment against a white literary tradition, however, is not to free oneself from white tradition but to face the whiteness of the American avant-garde. (For people who ask why more writers of color do not write "experimental fiction," this may get at why.) Experimentalism is experimental with regard to a specific tradition. Asian American fiction, for example, has its own tradition and experiments, into which an Asian American writer enters—if she is able to see that tradition as a possibility. If only one tradition is taught, some writers will always find more possibilities than others. This chapter will briefly go into one example of another craft tradition—the one closest to my heart: Asian American literature—but can only do so in a cursory way. It's impossible to trace an entire tradition, including its experiments, in a single essay—this is the point. Writers must read much more widely and much more deeply, if we are to know enough craft to start to critique other writers fairly and to write truly for ourselves.

For historical help, I will rely on the book *Chinese Theories of Fiction*, by Ming Dong Gu, which is the rare book that attempts a systematic classification of Chinese narrative theory—in English, by a scholar of Chinese descent. Most of the field of Chinese narrative theory is written by white scholars. Scholars of the Chinese diaspora have tended to focus on historical perspectives and/or studies of individual classic works. Gu himself is forced to spend chunks of his book pointing out this lack. In order to move his field forward, he first has to take it apart by showing that many leading white scholars have misunderstood, or even ignored, Chinese narratological tradition. He quotes Western scholars' claims that Chinese fiction includes an "undefinable inadequacy" and is "vaguely wanting." Gu argues that what Western scholars see as idiosyncrasies are not inadequacies; rather, "they are characteristic features that grew out of the philosophical, social, cultural, and aesthetic conditions" of a distinctly Chinese narratological tradition.

Gu is fantastically categorical. He lists ten ways in which Chinese tradition is different from Western tradition: (1) Chinese fiction comes from street talk and gossip, not the epic or the romance; (2) the main narrative might be accompanied by commentary from another fictional character included or not in the story; (3) the narrator or author can interrupt at any time and point out the fictionality of the work (as in metafiction); (4) the author and reader may show up within the story as themselves (sometimes associated with postmodernism); (5) the inclusion of multiple unreliable narrators; (6) the fantastic is a part of the everyday world (as in magical realism); (7) intertextuality, especially the inclusion of poems and songs; (8) multiple conflicting points of view; (9) episodic structure; and (10) a mix of formal language with vernacular or even vulgar language.

Some of these characteristics are found in Western fiction but have been anticipated by Chinese writers hundreds of years earlier. The foundational difference is that Chinese fiction has always existed in opposition to historical narrative. History recorded the official versions; fiction, when it was recorded, were the stories common folk told each other, the unofficial versions, and reflect this in their craft. In this context, for example, it makes sense for Chinese fiction to insist that any narrative has a teller and that the teller may or may not be reliable—and to include multiple tellers. The vulgarity and vernacular may also be meant to disrupt official storytelling.

Asian American fiction often contains a similar challenge to official history. When I teach Asian American literature or Asian American Studies, there are always some students who have never heard of the incarceration of Japanese Americans during World War II (I have stopped being surprised by this), and if they have heard of it, the narrative they know is usually that Japanese Americans went smilingly into these camps as a way to prove their Americanness. In fact, there was resistance, including violent resistance, and extreme internal and external conflict. Japanese American fiction often records stories of deep struggle before, during, and after the incarceration. The Asian American classic *No-No Boy* is about a man who said no to the two "loyalty questions" that prisoners were given (one whether they would give up Japanese citizenship—though it was illegal for Japanese immigrants, mostly parents, to become American citizens—and the other whether they would fight in the War, on the American side of course). In *No-No Boy*, Ichiro has just gotten out of prison after the War and has returned to Seattle, where he is mostly treated terribly. The novel often goes from third person to first person, as he argues with himself. In addition, there is the perspective of his friend Kenji, who fought in the War and was injured—fatally, it turns out. Ichiro and Kenji seem to function as two sides of the same person, as is often pointed out by literary critics. Like traditional Chinese fiction, the novel is criticized for its "flat" characters and for its mix of more formal language with the vernacular. (It is also praised for these things, depending on the critic.)

These aren't, of course, exactly the same tradition, but say for instance that an Asian American writer wanted to counter the stories told about her, about her identity, about her parents' identities, about her place in historical narrative. This is where my interest lies. When in the Western canon we encounter strategies like the interrupting author or commentary from other characters, it's often as part of the postmodernist project of finally challenging the earlier (perceived) authority and authenticity of the author. These models are not the best for an Asian American writer. In fiction like that by David Foster

Wallace or Paul Auster, political critique is hidden in intellectual critique, consideration of privilege is rare, race is mostly ignored. In the tradition of Asian American literature, resistance is a part of the canon (to the point that fiction that less models resistance may be too easily dismissed), and novels like *The Woman Warrior*, by Maxine Hong Kingston, or *No-No Boy*, or *Dogeaters*, by Jessica Hagedorn, regularly explore the question of what is "real" vs. "what is the movies"; disrupt authorial authenticity and/or presence; include other narrators with conflicting points of view; make the fantastic part of the everyday world; contain intertextuality; offer unofficial stories as primary sources of information; distrust official narrative; etc. To know the history is to know one's experience of being and speaking in the world is not alone. It is to know what conversations are open to you and your work. It is to know a certain audience.

For Asian American writers, here are some other things one might find useful in the model of traditional Chinese fiction:

1. Telling has priority over showing.
2. The plot structure follows kishotenketsu, which does not require conflict and is a four-act structure rather than a three-act (or five-act) structure. Instead of beginning, middle,

and ending (a beginning in which conflict is introduced, a middle in which conflict is faced, an ending in which conflict is resolved), ki is introduction, sho is development, ten is twist, and ketsu is reconciliation. Conflict is not necessary.

3. Poetry has a large influence on fiction, and some stories follow the structure of what Gu calls the "poetic sandwich," which means the story begins and ends with a poem.

4. Chinese fiction is not afraid of intense emotion. Rather than "showing" the emotion, such as through what T. S. Eliot called the "objective correlative" (for example: pouring water into a cup until it overflows to show sadness or an angel statue with its wings cut off to show the feeling of being trapped), melodrama (see: Asian dramas in which a situation is manufactured to make viewers feel something, such as sudden cancer or memory loss) is preferable. Writing meant to evoke a reaction from the audience rather than to represent an individual character is good craft.

5. Interiority, however, is not especially prized. There is an aesthetic commitment to, according to scholar Andrew Plaks, "an implicit understanding . . . that the causes of human

behavior usually need not be spelled out, or are better left unsaid." These gaps where interiority might tell us a character's motivations are purposefully omitted. Note that this is not emotion, but what we think as we do things. Any writer always leaves room for her readers, and this is a choice about where to leave that room.

6. Gu says Chinese fiction emphasizes "patterns of texture rather than of structure." What he means by this is that a story can be structured according to theme—exactly what Aristotle did not like about the episodic plot. Things can progress according to associative logic rather than cause and effect.

7. A "kaleidoscopic" quality (Gu) can be created from the pattern-based structure, or from an episodic plot, or from multiple narrators, or so forth, and represents a view of life that has more emphasis on multiplicity than individuality.

8. In Western fiction we have "dramatic irony," which is when the audience knows something that the characters do not. Perhaps the opposite of dramatic irony is "romantic irony" (coined by scholar Ralph Freedman), which is when the author creates the effect that there is no separation between audience and

characters, real world from fictional world. This can be achieved via intrusions by an author character and a reader character and via framing devices and stories within stories and the constant questioning of what is real and authentic both in fiction and in life.

9. Lastly, Gu shares other Chinese narrative theorists' observation that oneness, as in Buddhist philosophy, informs all of this craft, including something like "romantic irony" (in which the fiction and the author and the readers are all one). Nothing is separate or individual from anything else. No one lives or acts, or reads or writes, alone.

Part 2

WORKSHOP IN
THE REAL WORLD

"THE READER" VS. POC

In the traditional workshop model formalized in the 1940s and '50s and still popular among MFA programs, a group of the writer's peers discuss her work while she listens in silence. (Sometimes the writer's peers even refer to her as "the writer" and not by name, as if they do not know her and she is not in the room.) The idea is, as author Peter Turchi puts it, "to reflect the intention of the work back to" the writer. In other words, other writers reveal to the real author their understanding of the implied author (see the chapter "Audience, Theme, and Purpose" for more on the difference between the real and implied author). The "gag rule" that silences the author allows a discussion of the implied author that is supposedly free from the influence of the real author.

The usefulness of this workshop model relies on two premises: (1) that the real author is partly in the dark with regard to her work—or at least with regard to her subconscious intentions and their meaning—and (2) that the workshop can offer an interpretation of the work that will help the author to see either what she is already doing or what she might do instead.

In a silent workshop (especially one with no written or spoken introduction to the work from the author), readers must create a sense of the author's intentions from unfinalized craft choices. In other words, the workshop must first imagine a possible final draft, and only then—from this product of their *own* imagination, not the author's—critique its implied author.

Workshopping is necessarily an act of the imagination—and this is no easy task. If the benefit of workshop is *in* the act of imagining what could be from what is, then we must look for ways to make the task less hazardous and more potentially useful.

Starting with how we talk about "the reader."

Here is a thought experiment. If you have a workshop of twelve students with similar backgrounds—say twelve cis straight able Christian white men in their mid to late twenties all from the suburbs, whose parents all went to college, who all like *The Simpsons*, who read primarily American literary fiction, etc.—and one of them submits a story about a cis straight able Christian white man in his mid-twenties from a suburb who meets a cis straight able Christian white woman in her mid-twenties from a suburb, then who is "the reader" the workshop will imagine? We can imagine that "the reader" will be a lot like them—and also, since the author is a lot like them, a lot like the author. This particular workshop's task—to imagine the final version of the story according to the conventions of craft that come from a culture of Western psychological literary realism—may actually be relatively doable. Say the story begins with the man going out after his job teaching high school English and drinking away his stress in the neighborhood bar with a group of straight guy friends. In the bar is also a group of straight girl friends, and the group of guys know one of the women but not the others. The two groups join up and the main characters couple off. The woman is clearly not having the best time, and together the main characters step outside and have a conversation that draws them closer and allows the man to understand that he wasn't having the best time either; in fact, he's kind of depressed. Their friends keep pushing them toward one another, and eventually the two go home together. The next morning, the man wakes up happy for once and decides to skip work, but the woman rushes off and leaves him alone. Etc. Near the beginning of the story, the sentences jump around to various memories, but as the story gets going, things are pretty straightforward, until the tone turns suddenly lyrical at the end and everything works itself up to some sense of meaning.

The workshop of twelve middle-class cis straight white men who share similar expectations might have various things to say about this story, but one can imagine general agreement. The main points of contention are likely to be the changes in style and tone, and perhaps someone will suggest greater stakes and conflict and something to punch up the plot a bit. The writer goes home and adds a sick dog given to the male protagonist by his college girl-friend, the one who got away. The dog vomits on the bathroom floor while the man is out drinking, and after the woman leaves in the morning, the man finds the vomit on the floor and cleans it up very symbolically. Etc. The dog gives the story the chance to tie the man's memories to something concrete and offers more of what the workshop wanted.

This is no great story, of course. But it may be a fairly uncontentious story in this particular workshop. It may be read fairly similarly to the author's intentions, since those intentions also match the workshop's expectations, and the critique might go generally smoothly.

Now say the workshop is more mixed. In particular, it includes some women writers and writers who have some familiarity with gender studies, and the workshop gets on the topic of the representation of women in the story—mostly as objects and as vaguely in competition with each other and as sources of male lack, with one symbolized via a dog. It's the same story, so why does this workshop read it differently? Because it is a different audience. This time the workshop is more critical and at the end the author says nothing and either decides to incorporate the suggestions or dismisses them as not of his concern. Why one or the other? Because he believes the critique comes either from his audience or not from his audience.

Now say the workshop has students of color in it,

students with disabilities, queer students, students from other socioeconomic classes and religions and countries. If they feel free to talk, the workshop is even less agreeable, and now the sticking point is the fact that the story seems to exist in a cultural bubble. The representations of women, the lack of geographical and cultural specificity, the lack of diversity, the conformity to a certain kind of literary story, the extremely low stakes of a protagonist who really does not have much trouble in his life, etc. The workshop complains that the guy seems totally unlikeable, unrelatable; the premise itself seems uninteresting; the prose, for the most part, is dull. Maybe the one spot where the workshop sees creative possibility is in the jumping memories toward the beginning of the story, which disappear as things get going.

Again the difference is audience. At the end of *this* workshop, the author is stewing and angry and perhaps tries to defend himself, etc. He goes home and either decides to start over or dismisses the comments as not of his concern . . . because he believes the critique comes either from his audience or not from his audience at all.

Which audience are we? MFA workshops are infamous for being mostly white, mostly cis, mostly straight, mostly able, mostly middle-class, mostly literary and realist. The writers who face the biggest gap between the expectations of the workshop and the expectations of their actual audience are marginalized writers: writers of color, LGBTQ+ writers, disabled writers, working-class writers, non-literary-realist writers, etc. On top of that, the academic and publishing worlds constantly reinforce dominant norms by which books get published or celebrated, which writers get teaching jobs, etc. In this culture, who is "the reader" the workshop will imagine?

I graduated with my MFA in 2009 and my PhD in 2016 and, as of the writing of this book, have taught over sixty workshops. As a student, I took fourteen workshops of varying quality. One professor said that if I wanted to experiment, I was in the wrong place. On the other hand, my thesis advisor, Margot Livesey, taught me much of what I still know about craft in the tradition of psychological literary realism. What my peers and I consistently valued from our instructors was an instructor's ability to see our stories as we meant them. Margot was remarkably good at this. I wrote only one story she didn't "get." It was the one that came closest to the material of my adoption.

For a long time, I wondered both how she saw our intentions so well, especially when many of our backgrounds were so different from hers, and why she didn't see my intentions in that particular story. This is not criticism—it is an attempt to put what Margot taught me into practice for myself. After my first two years of teaching, I spent part of a writing conference asking how other authors run their workshops. Eventually, the author Nami Mun explained to me that she leads each workshop differently since each story is different. To hear it put so plainly stunned me. This was an extension of what Margot had done for us, to read each story on its own terms. In my next course, I started employing the gag rule only in certain workshops, in certain situations, or skipping discussion to map structure on the wall, or asking my students to each draw their own version of the story, or so on and so forth.

But I was still teaching largely homogenous classes: cis straight able middle-class white women. Every once in a while, when a story led to a contentious discussion about race, I would find myself both professionally empowered and racially disempowered. I was supposed to lead critique, but I was also obviously outside of the author's audience.

Typically, when fiction writers employ the term "the reader," they do so to refer to a generalized reader (not a specific or even an *intended* one). This means that the term rarely makes a distinction between a male reader or a female reader, a white reader or a Black reader, a cis straight reader or an LGBTQ+ reader—and even acts as a shield sometimes for the person talking. To refer to "the reader" in this way is to flatten audience to a single group of readers who share a single group of cultural expectations. Different readerships are overlooked or othered, the result of which is to make difference an exception. Difference becomes a burden, one that falls upon writers already burdened by their difference in the world.

As craft is a set of expectations, the workshop needs to know which expectations, whose expectations, the author wishes to engage with, if the workshop is to imagine useful possibilities for the story. And if the main benefit of workshop is reading stories in progress/process, then we need to acknowledge and utilize the benefit of hearing about that process. Why do we let this opportunity go when it can be used to *better* interpret a story? To silence the author is to willingly misinterpret the author. It is to insist that she must write *to the workshop*.

A useful workshop considers who "the reader" is for each particular writer and therefore approaches each particular story on its own terms. Otherwise, intentions are not reflected back to the author but forced on her. A common complaint about the proliferation of MFA programs is that they breed generic writing. The real danger is not a single style, it's a single audience. It is effectively a kind of colonization to assume that we all write for the same audience or that we should do so if we want our fiction to sell. When the workshop critiques a manuscript from the position of an unspecified, and therefore normative, reader—or when it similarly claims "universal" values as if values are not cultural—it makes fiction's greatest strength its greatest weakness. It demands from the imagination either conformity or exoticism. The result, for marginalized writers in particular, is work that is no longer its author's. It is work that speaks, at best, to the workshop and, at worst, to no one at all.

WHO IS AT THE CENTER OF WORKSHOP AND WHO SHOULD BE?

While I was still in my PhD program, I did a panel at a local book festival with another writer from the program and a writer who was considering a PhD. When we asked why she was hesitating, she said she hated workshops. My colleague nodded understandingly and said he hated workshops too. I didn't know what to say. We all had MFAs and two of us had gone back for more, and yet it seemed like a dangerously unpopular opinion, after all that, to still believe in workshopping. Many writers seem to come out of MFA programs not only hating workshop but thinking that they are *supposed* to hate workshop, as if hating it is part of the workshop's design.

That semester, I was teaching two workshops, and with one, I tried something I had never done before. After workshopping everyone once during the first half of the course, we spent the second half of the term on revision workshops, following a completely different workshop model. In the revision workshops, the author's peers were only allowed to ask her questions, not offer any suggestions or criticism. I especially encouraged questions in the form of what-ifs.

Here are some examples I gave them:

- Why does the backstory on page 3 come so early? How would the story change if it came later?
- Why does this story progress in achronological order? What would the story be like if it didn't?
- Why does the mother suddenly slap her son? What would the story be like if she hugged him?
- How does the son know that the father is going to leave the family? What if it was a surprise?

Their questions were supposed to be:

a. questions the workshopper did not already know the answer to—i.e., not evaluative statements in the form of questions;

b. not simply matters of information (such as "How old is the narrator?"); and

c. designed to get the *author* to think rather than to share the thoughts of the workshopper.

I tried this model out for several reasons. First, though I have been in multiple workshops where later sessions focus on revision, often the same ground is covered, with the workshop leader using similar techniques, which makes those sessions feel repetitive or, even worse, redundant. Second, I wanted to prioritize process (why and how the author made the changes she made). Third, I wanted the writer, as she revised, to become more conscious of all the decisions she made—why she added backstory about the mother character, for example, or why she cut the next-door neighbor—and how she came to those decisions and how the decisions affected other decisions, etc. Fourth, I wanted to give my students the tools to revise beyond the workshop, when one has to ask and answer for/to oneself. Many students seem flummoxed by what comes next and how to know what questions to ask themselves, how to train themselves to ask the right questions. Fifth, the typical workshop doesn't center the author of the workshop manuscript, even without the cone of silence. As one of my MFA professors used to warn, workshop is most helpful to whoever speaks the most, not to the person being workshopped.

Indeed I have found this warning to be overwhelmingly accurate. Workshop's greatest pedagogical value is in its ability to help writers clarify their own aesthetics (often referred to as "finding their voice"). But this work does not happen in silence. You clarify your aesthetics by talking and writing about how you believe fiction should work and what you believe fiction should do (that is, by actively engaging with the cultural expectations you have learned and are learning). When the author is allowed to speak, and can steer the conversation, the workshop dynamic does change—getting rid of the gag rule can help set parameters on feedback and make that feedback more helpful—but the way we talk about craft can still feel more like a press conference than a process.

Partly the decentering of the author is built into the design of how we teach writing. Student writers are taught to analyze fiction for what they themselves can learn from it—often called "reading like a writer"—rather than from what the author has or is learning from it. This way of reading has its uses, but it also has its problems. Especially when the workshop is ostensibly meant to address the author's own manuscript and writing. And especially when we factor in the usual power dynamics in the usual workshop (white, straight, cis, able, male, middle-class, etc.)—I'll come back to this.

In addition, workshop is incredibly persuasive, as power usually is. I remember being a student in a novel workshop that seemed to change every manuscript for the worse, because the writers listened too much to too many suggestions, and telling myself I would never make the same mistake. But two years later, I had to throw out my entire manuscript and start over. As much as I had tried to resist falling into the same trap, ultimately writing is about an audience, and you're never closer to *an* audience than when the workshop tells you exactly what it wants. I had tried to satisfy the desires of people who were actually working out for themselves their own desires, and therefore had taken on the concerns of other novels as my own.

If I seem so far to agree with the other two writers on my panel—to hate workshops—I should stop here to acknowledge that talking about other people's works in progress really did teach me a lot. In the novel workshop I mentioned, I learned a lot about how a certain kind of novel works and that my idea of a novel was very different from that convention. That was an important lesson. It's just that my own particular work in progress suffered, because it was decentered by the nature of the workshop.

It took me many years to find the center again.

Let me be clear about the benefits of critiquing someone else's story: If we in fact critique other people's writing through our own writing perspective, that critique helps us to understand ourselves. Since the weaknesses we perceive in a manuscript are weaknesses *we perceive*, our solutions might be most helpful to the problems we face in our own work. But one writer's treasure is another writer's trash. In the two years I spent writing myself out of my novel, I wasn't aware of what I was doing. I could tell I was getting good advice—I couldn't tell that it was good advice for someone else.

Now take this inherent decentering of the author and enter race, gender, sexuality, ability, class, and so forth. For more privileged writers, their decentering in workshop is countered by their centering in the rest of the world. A cis able white male who leaves workshop feeling disempowered usually finds the rest of his American life more than willing to empower him again. Someone less privileged leaves a disempowering workshop and faces the same disempowerment on a larger scale: though they should be in charge of their story, they are again made to listen to other people telling them what their story is or should be. The result is exactly the opposite of finding their voice—the real-world silencing simply reinforces the idea that the marginalized writer should be writing toward the workshop and power.

Defenders of the traditional model claim that decentering the author is a way of prioritizing audience, of talking about the story from a readerly perspective. (Such is often a goal of workshop.) But we need to think more about how and when to empower authors. And we need to talk more about power's relationship to audience (as marginalization only increases if it is unacknowledged or unchallenged). As this book has argued, the workshop isn't even necessarily an author's intended audience, a problem compounded by an unreflective use of "the reader" (see the previous chapter).

In other words, even when workshop is at its most effective, its effect is to mirror and implicitly endorse unequal power structures in the real world. Why do we cling to this outdated model?

When I asked my class to workshop the author solely via questions, it was my intent to move the center of the workshop from the workshoppers back to the author. My students seemed ready to embrace this shift wholeheartedly—I think that they wanted to—but in practice I encountered a lot of resistance. They found it difficult to center the author, to ask questions about the story rather than make assumptions, to ask what the author thought about potential issues rather than suggest how to "fix" those issues. I had to stop the workshop several times and redirect our efforts.

I had anticipated some trouble reversing the workshop model. I had built in a week where we looked at an early draft of one of my own stories and also the finished, published draft, and they practiced asking questions on me. I was hesitant to bring my own work into the classroom, but I thought it might prepare them to ask and answer real questions of its real author in this very different kind of workshop.

Instead I discovered that, especially for the more talkative members of the workshop, they found it hard to decenter themselves as workshoppers. They were used to feeling ownership over the author's process. Even the authors felt this way—they were used to workshop taking the work out of their own hands. One student said it made her very uncomfortable to have to answer questions about her own story, rather than sit back and listen. But more than that, I think, they all had gone through many years of school where literature is discussed via interpretation: not by asking questions of the author, but by using the text to answer questions of our own.

In workshopping via only questions, I had meant to interrogate process—the one thing workshop offers us that literary analysis usually does not—I had meant to let the author work out for herself what to do with her story, not give persuasive power to other people's readings. I wonder whether my students' attachment to the cone-of-silence model was precisely *because* it mimics the real-world power situation. In the world, the majority holds power and we are expected to know its norms. I wonder, too, whether the cone of silence actually encourages writers to think that this is the way life should be—that the person who should benefit most from speaking is the person who has the most power to speak. I wonder, in other words, whether we shortchange our students in terms of their real lives to run a workshop that decenters the lone voice and instead centers the majority.

I believe in workshop as a shared act of imagination, in the ability of many minds to foster the growth of one by one by one through conversation. I believe in the vulnerability of process and the process of vulnerability. I wouldn't write this book if I didn't. But if we are to use workshop as a pedagogical approach, we need to actively acknowledge and confront the dangers of workshop both to the writing itself—if "writing itself" even exists—and to our personhoods.

It is instructors' responsibility to remake things—and that starts with burning the old models down. In retrospect, a question-based workshop was probably such a difficult transition for my class because we didn't first do enough of the very necessary work of naming and unmaking the dynamics of the typical workshop. It is hard to go from being the center to centering someone else. We see this truth every day. It is difficult to give up power. Students have been taught to give up their power when they sit in the author's seat, so they are willing to do that. They haven't been taught to give up the power of the majority. I have done better since at preparing my students to engage with different expectations—it can be done. The following chapter will present some alternative workshop models, including my current one. Some of these alternatives I have experimented with directly and others I have not. But not knowing how these strategies might work is surely a big reason the traditional workshop persists. We know it. If we must be willing to risk ourselves in our writing, we must be willing to risk ourselves in how we teach writing. It is time for workshop to change.

ALTERNATIVE WORKSHOPS

1. Critical Response Process

Critical Response Process was developed by artist Liz Lerman and is mostly used for performance and theater arts. But it works for any creative art and is gaining popularity in creative writing workshops. The process consists of four steps:

1. Observations (what Lerman calls "Statements of Meaning") designed for the author to hear how the workshop reacted to the work.
2. Questions from the artist to the workshop.
3. Questions from the workshop to the artist—these are supposed to be "neutral," by which Lerman means, without opinion.
4. Suggestions (what Lerman calls "Opinion Time")—if the artist gives permission.

2. Modified CRP

I often use a modified version of CRP as a starting point, from which the workshop may diverge according to the particular needs of the author and manuscript. The basic steps are below. I will go into more detail at the end of this chapter, especially regarding what students do with the workshop manuscripts before workshop even starts. Of note is that about half of the workshops in any course I teach end up doing something other than this modified CRP. If you are interested in how I pick different approaches for different stories, some of the individual options are listed later in this chapter as "Author-Choice Workshops."

Here are the basic steps of modified CRP:

a. The author submits the workshop manuscript with "Writing Notes" that describe her process, her intended audience, and any craft decisions she made while writing and revising the manuscript.

b. The workshop describes what they have read (such as: the audience and how the author addresses that audience, what kind of story the story is, its shape or tone or so forth, what the story is "about," genres and craft traditions within which the story is working, etc.). This is not summary or criticism but transparency

about the ways the workshop has already con-
structed the story in its imagination.

c.   The author responds to the description and
poses a question or multiple questions that
frame the discussion that follows.

d.   Discussion includes questions from both the author and the workshop. This is a conversation—
readers are not allowed to say what they have
already written in their peer letters.

e.   The workshop offers what-ifs and suggestions
specific to each page.

f.   The author ends by naming one or two things
she will try next in revision.

3. Partner-Led Workshops

In this model writers are paired up for the course according to aesthetic similarities or differences and are
in constant communication with each other about their
manuscripts. Before workshop, they should meet and discuss particular concerns, fears, desires, etc. for workshop
and come up with a plan for how best to approach the
story. (A lot of instructor-work is necessary to prepare the
workshop for this task—when I lead workshops this way, I
check in with each pair every week and sometimes before
workshop to discuss the approach we will take in class).
The author's partner should then lead discussion, taking
questions and redirecting and adding commentary when
necessary.

4. Only Questions from the Workshop

The workshop asks questions of the author, and nothing else, which the author may choose to answer or simply note. Questions in this kind of workshop require a lot of preparation, so that workshoppers understand and believe in the kind of questions that do not couch opinion. Sometimes, as in Jesse Ball's model, The Asking, which is based on a Quaker tradition, partners may be used to moderate, which again seems to work best when the partners meet before the workshop and discuss in depth the author's concerns both about the workshop and about the story. If not the author's partner, the instructor should meet with the author beforehand and moderate the workshop.

5. Only Questions from the Author

In this model, the workshop sends the marked-up manuscripts and their feedback letters to the author before the workshop begins—at least a couple of days before, but earlier might be preferable. The author reads everything and formulates questions about topics to expand on, ways to approach revision, readerly reactions, etc. In workshop, the author leads the discussion by asking questions that the workshop answers. In my experience, students are eager to try this method, but it works better for advanced students who are more equipped to answer follow-up questions to their critiques. Instructor help is needed to keep this kind of workshop in conversation, rather than in multiple one-on-one interactions between the author and specific peers. Encourage the author to think beyond simply getting clarification. Instead, it should be a way for the author to open doors that they now know exist but do not know where they lead.

6. Only Suggestions from the Author

As in the previous model, the author reviews all feed-back days before workshop. She then generates a list of "suggestions," which consists of changes, additions, and cuts she might make. This list should be possible but not definite—in other words, the suggestions may be things the author has only vaguely thought about or things the author has thought a lot about, but shouldn't be things the author will definitely do with revision. (It helps to encourage the author to go big, to write down things she might never otherwise attempt, to encourage her to think of the workshop as a way to test out wild ideas.) Ideally, this is a model in which the author imagines the possible versions of the story and the workshop discusses them. Workshop consists of talking through the author's list. This is meant to prepare the author for revision. It's also a good way to build confidence and get writers excited about going back to work on their manuscripts.

7. Everyone Workshops at the Same Time

I have run this kind of workshop in two different cir-cumstances: for novels and for stories guided by in-class prompts (so that everyone in the workshop writes a story and revises it with the same prompts). I have found that this results in very little criticism and a lot of learning from each other's processes. In the novel workshop, we did this by talking each day about a different element of the novel and how the writers in workshop approached that element. For example, we might talk about plot, various models of plot, how plot works in the novel manuscripts, what troubles each writer might be having with plot, what the writers learned from each other, successes in each other's work, etc. For the prompt-guided stories, everyone began with the same extended prompt and we talked about how each writer approached that prompt differently, what strategies they used, what they could learn from each other and their differences, what went well in the process and what didn't, and then we chose together something to do in revision; this continued with each week.

This kind of workshop takes the burden off of a single writer at a time and gives everything a more collaborative feel. It requires a lot of preparation from the instructor, and sometimes a good deal of coaxing from the instructor to keep the conversation going. However, these have been some of the most constructive, encouraging, and useful workshops I have run. Generally for more advanced writers.

8. Flipped Workshop

A flipped classroom is a simple idea, but is sometimes very difficult to pull off. It means that the work that is usually done in class, such as discussion and lecture, is done outside of class, and the work that is usually done outside of class, such as writing and reading, is done in class. I have used Google Docs for flipped workshops, but other programs would work. In this model, writers workshop their manuscripts online. (The instructor should monitor the work being done.) One advantage is that more stories can be workshopped each week, though of course this also means a greater time commitment. It also allows shyer students to contribute more.

In class, writers might address lingering questions, as in the fourth model here, or talk through or work on revision. Writers might discuss their revisions or their workshops in groups or meet with the instructor one-on-one. The instructor can offer prompts and exercises based on specific concerns from the online workshops and can then give immediate feedback on process. Usually, I have had writers revise in class, whether through exercises or otherwise. For example, they might reorganize their story physically and tape it to sections of the wall, so that everyone can walk around. Or they might work on a specific task, such as verb choices, and then share the results with the class.

9. Author-Choice Workshops

Each author chooses the parameters of her own workshop—what is permissible and not permissible, what kind of feedback to give, the order of events, the setup of the classroom, etc. The instructor should provide options such as the ones on this list and also open the floor to any additional options that might come up. (I have also chosen these options for students who might be better served by one of these models than by the modified CRP we start with.) Once, a friend told me that when she let her students decide how their workshops would go, one student wanted everyone to lie on the floor, so that no one could see anyone else. This model can also be modified to fall within certain options or guidelines, or to determine specific parts of workshop, such as feedback letters or how to begin the workshop. In partner workshops, the author's partner might make interesting choices, especially for partners who work well together.

Possible choices for individual workshops:

a. *Scissors and Tape*: Cut up the manuscript and tape it to the wall. There are various ways to approach this. The manuscript might be cut up to separate scene from summary, to separate present story from backstory, to cut up main plot from subplots, to follow certain characters, to follow certain themes, etc. Helpful at first is to tape up the manuscript as it currently stands, simply cut into the separate sections, and arrange it with each page as a column. Then move the pieces around, but keep the page order: perhaps keep the present story on the top and put the backstory near the bottom of each column. This example presents a visual representation of how much present story and backstory is on each page, and how that proportion changes as the story moves along. Finally, move the pieces into new positions, asking what each move might mean, asking where the author and/or workshop would move pieces, etc. The instructor might lead this process, or the author, or the author's partner, or each member of workshop might make their own arrangement.

b. *Draw the Story*: Everyone draws a pictorial representation of the story (keep this vague, as some writers may draw the structure, some the themes, etc., and the differences are useful). These drawings are shared and explained. The author may ask questions.

c. *Map the Story*: Similar to B, except that everyone draws a "map" of the story. After individual explanations and questions, the workshop as a whole might work together with the author to create a map of what possible finished versions of the story might look like.

d. *Sticky Notes*: Sometimes called "sweeping" (a term I've heard attributed to Amy Hempel), start by identifying various elements on each page. This may utilize different-color sticky notes, such as one color for characters, one color for themes, one color for plot developments, one color for stakes, etc. Arrange these notes at first in the order they appear, in columns to represent each page. This should present imbalances that are either useful or not so useful to the story. Now talk through moving various elements around to where they might be most useful to the story. (Instead of sticky notes, I have used colored paper and markers so that the workshop can read the "notes" from their seats.)

e. *Highlighters and Underlining*: Have everyone highlight or underline various things in the manuscript. I've found this particularly useful with "inside story" and "outside story" or "character arc" and "story arc," with identifying characterization or agency or stakes or so on in the story, and with stylistic matters. Also with identifying shifts in tense, POV, time (especially a lot of shifts in time, even in individual sentences and paragraphs). Again, this is useful in giving the author (and workshop) a visual way of understanding her manuscript. Stylistically, each writer might highlight sentences that best represent the author's style and underline sentences that least represent the author's style (with explanations for what the style is and why these specific sentences) or so forth.

f. *T Charts or Venn Diagrams*: These can be used to compare the beginning to the ending, one character to another, inside and outside story, an earlier draft to a later draft, etc. For example, I often use T charts to show how two different characters in a story might present two different models for the protagonist (the obvious one: mom and dad). One friend might have ended up a lawyer and unhappy while another friend might have ended up broke but content. A Venn diagram might be more useful if you also want to highlight common attributes, such as things the two friends have in common also with the protagonist, like where they grew up and how they all wanted at one time to be rock stars, in the same band, etc.

g. *The Hot Seat*: Someone other than the author sits in the workshop's "hot seat." This could be a partner who acts as the author, other workshoppers (alone or in rotation), or the instructor. For example, the instructor might attempt to defend the choices the author made (based on the evidence of prior meetings, the manuscript, and/or notes on the writer's process), which can give the author and the workshop a sense of how each craft decision has meaning and consequence and can acquire conscious intention. Alternatively, the person in the hot seat could be a character (this works well with younger writers) who might be asked to explain why she did certain things in the story or what her life looks like otherwise or so on. The author or partner could answer for the character.

10. *Defense-Style*

As in a thesis or dissertation defense, the author might first present a defense of her various craft decisions, explaining why she did certain things in the story and what they mean, even going line by line. This can be done with a "committee" made up of readers who have seen more than one draft and an "audience" made up of the rest of the workshop, or it can be done with the whole class. The workshop should ask questions that help the author clarify her intentions. However, this model needs a lot of preparation and a lot of counteracting the power imbalance that occurs (also in a thesis/dissertation defense) when the author must be "on defense" against the feeling of being attacked.

11. *Author-as-Workshopper*

This is the reverse of the defense-style workshop. In this model, the author critiques the story, and the workshop attempts to defend it. This can be especially useful when the author already has a good idea of what she thinks the flaws in her manuscript are, and when workshop might simply repeat her concerns back to her. When the workshop defends the manuscript, they are put in the position of the author, and the author may learn new possibilities for the story and for how to think about the things she currently feels are flaws.

12. Debate-Style

The author submits a list of craft decisions she made in the story, along with her manuscript, and the workshop splits in half. Half the workshop defends the author's decisions while the other half critiques them. The author may moderate or defer to a partner or the instructor to moderate.

13. Elements of Fiction

This model is particularly useful in beginner workshops. From a list of various elements of fiction that the workshop has already discussed and/or is familiar with (plot, scene, structure, setting, characterization, etc.), writers randomly select one element to talk about. (Perhaps they draw from a hat.) The selection may be done on the spot (which means workshoppers should be familiar with any and all terms) or before the workshop (which allows workshoppers to prepare their remarks). Workshop covers these various elements in the particular workshop manuscript, each element led by a single participant.

Alternatively, this model can be done in subgroups, wherein each group workshops a different element (or elements) in the story and then summarizes their conversation in the larger workshop. However, this cuts off some of the author's access to the particularities of each discussion (for good or ill).

14. *Workshop the Workshop*
After workshopping a manuscript, the workshop workshops the workshop. That is, they discuss what seemed to go well or poorly in the workshop, how they could do better, etc. This model contributes to improved workshops as a course goes on.

SYLLABUS EXAMPLE

The following is how I explain my basic model of workshop for students, which is a modified version of the Critical Response Process. This is syllabus language, so the audience is student writers and not instructors. Workshop leaders might find it useful to modify or adapt this language to their own use. Some of the language below I first adapted in 2012 from a syllabus shared with me by friend and author Chip Cheek, one of many examples I have drawn from over the years.

·

1. Writing Notes
Each student will write detailed Writing Notes. In these Notes you should reflect on your writing decisions. The Notes should describe your thinking as you apply the exercises and as you consider the readings, discussions, and lessons. For your workshop manuscript, you should describe your process, your intentions, the difficulties you

faced, your audience, etc. Basically, you should reflect on your aesthetics as a writer, what you want to do with your writing and how and why.

Updated Writing Notes should be dated and turned in weekly via the course page. You will be graded on completion and thoroughness. These notes are for your own use, so they don't need to be grammatically correct or so forth; they should help you understand what kind of writer you are and *want to be/become*, by examining where you added writing or deleted writing and why, why a character does one thing and not another and what that means, what your evolving idea of your story and audience is, what you think are your strengths and weaknesses, etc. BE AS SPECIFIC AS POSSIBLE.

To help you get a sense of what to do in your Notes, here's an example from a past student:

> In class, I had to map out the relationships of the characters in a family tree, and the names were too confusing. I want to make the story accessible to someone with a limited attention span. So the first thing I did was open a new page and write the story from scratch using a simplified list of characters but the same overall plot structure. Intro to the scenery, we're in his/my Aunt's house, the funeral is the same but instead of a great uncle it's a grandfather, etc. I just wrote it straight through,

pacing this second version of the story very similarly to the first. As the notes I made in class re: suspense included adding dialogue and "hints," I made an effort as I reread the story I put together today—what I wrote in class was more like a hodgepodge of ideas, but this version was very much based on those notes with some language transferred over directly—and make my character more obviously critical, snarky, arrogant. I tried to do this by adding some internal monologue, writing in the first person, and creating the conversation with his sister, which was inspired by the above (where I was trying out names like Sly, short for Sylvester, and Mandy). I don't think it's suspenseful yet, in that it's unclear still what the character's motivations are. Why does it matter to him that he be a good uncle all of a sudden, when the only real revelation he's had is that he doesn't feel as close to or similar to his sister (Percival's mom) as he does to his second cousins and great uncle? What helps his distain for his own nuclear family dissolve? What about his relationship with his dad? I think he wants to be the "Boppy" equivalent in Percival's life, to help the next generation escape the buttoned-up attitudes of his own childhood in any way he can, and the only way available to him at this moment is trains. I'll try to write that in for next time. Hopefully the trains will help give my audience something concrete to hold on to.

(shared with permission from
former student Catherine Blanchard)

For your workshop packet, attach all Writing Notes to the *end* of your manuscript. Do not put your Writing Notes at the beginning of the packet. Writing Notes can be especially helpful to the workshop as we think about the direction you're taking the story, who your audience may be, and where you were or weren't able to accomplish your goals. Make sure that you include these things, as this will greatly improve your workshop experience. The notes are NOT meant to be questions for the workshop, but a record of what you want to do with the story and how you tried to do it.

2. Workshop Guidelines

Every manuscript is a work in progress/in process. So workshop will be a space in which to talk about writing as a *process*. The workshop is a space uniquely situated to talk about unfinished work. That is its one major benefit, what it offers that reading published stories cannot.

Reading and making comments

You must read each manuscript twice. The first reading (do NOT mark up the text during this round) should be for pleasure and for general reaction. In fact, recording your first reaction might end up being just as important to the writer as the more detailed suggestions you should make upon second read.

After your first quick read, you should see some brief Writing Notes from the author. Read those, and then record your first reaction by writing a simple chart at the top of the first page of the packet. This should be very basic, not complete sentences. For example:

+	?
plot	stakes
character arc	POV
details	tone
structure	opening
ending	

(Your vocabulary will increase as the course goes on.)

The author's comments in her Writing Notes should situate us in the material as part of a process. During your *second read*, think about where the work is in that process. This is a good time to mark up the pages themselves, asking questions in the margins or in the space between lines. Don't overdo things—remember that the story and especially individual sentences will change a lot in revision. Use most of the margins to pose *specific questions* regarding *specific passages*, such as why the author uses this word or the character acts in that way.

Once you have read the story twice, write a letter for the author (you should go onto a second page double-spaced, at least). Type it up, since you will bring a copy for your instructor. Here is where you will address the larger issues.

NB: Do the macro work in the letter and the micro work in the margins.

We will focus our overall comments on *observations*, *questions*, and *possibilities* for revision. (You should think of possibilities as open doors. Or as closed doors that might be opened.) Observations will help us discuss and describe how the author's Notes matched up to the story. Questions will help the author to generate her own thoughts about her story. Possibilities for revision might take the form of suggestions, but would be better as what-ifs (e.g. what if this evil character had a really nice friend?) and should focus on process—things to *try*. More examples might be reordering events in chronological order, or shuffling them to represent the narrator's addled mindset.

In your letter, you should ask macro questions and point out macro opportunities. Which means, for example, you might state your understanding (or not) of the story, list observations that seem especially juicy, ask questions about what certain actions or images mean, ask questions about specific characters, open the door to new possibilities in the plot or arc or theme or so on, etc. *Never* skimp on the questions in favor of suggestions. Making observations and asking questions are more about the author; suggestions are more about the workshopper. We're trying to find a happy medium.

Half your letter (at least) should be questions—this will factor into grading.

Advice, part 1:

- To begin with, you should think about audience as you write and read, as you draft, as you do your Writing Notes, and as a workshopper (and in writing your letters to the author). Whom we are writing for is the main factor in the decisions we make in the text. Here's an example that includes my own blind spots: A science fiction story written for science fiction fans will vary greatly from a science fiction story written for "literary" fans, and the decisions the writer faces will then vary greatly as well. Literary sci-fi often has a lot less science and perhaps less fact-based science. It only gets more complicated when these concerns and questions of audience have to do with, say, writing about and/or for marginalized groups.
- Second, your regular workshop advice: Both in class and in your written comments, over-simplified statements such as "I liked it" or "I didn't like it" are NOT helpful. These aren't observations, they are opinions without analysis. Neither is "I agree" or "I disagree" helpful.

Nor is "I want" or "I would like to see." Never is "I relate to this" helpful—you are one specific reader, not the intended audience. See, later, "Banned from Workshop."

- Workshops operate on the golden-rule policy: do for others as you want for yourself. Your fellow classmates will see from your comments what kind of feedback to give no matter how much of a push the instructor gives. Another way to think about questions and possibilities is that it's about *why* and *how*. Instead of saying you liked this or didn't like that, make an observation about the style or conflict or plot, etc., and ask the author what she meant.

- *Be specific and precise*, and ask questions you don't know how to answer, and give suggestions that come from reading the story for what the author wants it to be, not what you want it to be.

- In class, it helps to direct the workshop toward specific places in the text—e.g., "Is the image in the second paragraph of page 3 supposed to get across Soo Young's emotional distress?" or "I noticed on page 3 that Alex is unusually reserved. What action might Soo Young do there to express her emotional distress?"

- Be honest and tactful and generous, and above all, be respectful of the writer's artistic effort as well as his/her feelings. *Critique should never be personal or damaging.*

- We are all trying to encourage each other to keep writing, and to keep improving. Again, revision is a continual process. We don't want to stop anyone in her tracks. This can't be stressed enough: workshop shouldn't be about how the workshopper would have written the story. The Notes should help immensely. Help the author to see the exciting possibilities in her story.

What will the workshop look like?

At the beginning of workshop, the author of the workshop manuscript will read her favorite one or two paragraphs. (Good practice reading—read **slowly**.) This will help to get us back under the spell of the story and allow us to hear the voice on the page as it sounds to the author. It will give us a sense of what the author thinks she is doing well. It is also nice to have a second of headspace.

Second, someone in class will describe the material. This description may include how the author is addressing her audience, what kind of story the story is and/or wants to be, what the story is "about," other texts you were reminded of, genres and traditions the work is operating in, etc. Do not summarize or criticize here. The description is a good way for the author to see what stands out in the draft and what might be less memorable, and to hear how other people read the work and interpreted the Writing Notes. Other students in the workshop will add to the description.

Third, after listening to this, the author should respond to the description and then *pose a question or questions*. Those questions will kick-start our discussion and help set its terms, and we will proceed with a more open conversation that should include asking the author direct questions, asking each other questions, and—if the author desires, and with the author's feedback—offering suggestions.

Finally, if there is time, we might flip through the pages and talk about specific places where we had observations or questions or saw other possibilities.

Remember that workshop is NOT a time to voice out loud the things you wrote in your letter—the author will read the letters separately. Like any good conversation, workshop should push things further and be responsive to questions and comments at hand.

If at any time the author feels like the workshop is getting away from more relevant concerns, the author should say she wants to "redirect" the workshop. (If it is too awkward to speak up, raise a hand.) She can then ask another question of us or reframe the discussion. At any time, the author should feel free to (and should!) ask questions. This is also on the instructor and workshop—we need to check in with the author. Remember that the author is in the room and that this is indeed a conversation, not talking at the author or talking as if she isn't there. The author should use her judgment in offering explanations: It might be best for her to put her explanations of what she was attempting to do in the Writing Notes and, in class, to give direct answers to the workshop's questions. The workshop should try to ask only questions that are not already answered in the manuscript or the Writing Notes.

We will run these workshops according to what might be most useful to the material and author at the center. This means that in some workshops, and at some points in workshop, the author might listen more or speak more, clarify more, ask more questions, lead or sit back. In most workshops, we will stray from this basic structure and do other things, such as demonstrating methods of revision. We will attempt to workshop each author in a way that fits her and her manuscript.

The author will likely want to take notes (though there is also the option to designate a specific person to take notes for the author, which can free her up to join more readily in the conversation, which we can discuss). Personally I find it helpful to quickly note what was said as well as who said it and any questions I might have, in case discussion is going well and I want to wait and bring up those questions later. Of course you should figure out a system of note-taking that works for you. It should go without saying that none of us should judge each other's note-taking systems (or coping strategies) during workshop.

At the end of her workshop, the author will be asked to state one or two things that she will try out in revision. For example, someone might have said something about a mother character holding the possibility for more conflict with her cruel family, and the author might say she has decided to reexamine the mother character and ask what it is in the mother's past or present that makes her so permissive. The author should walk out of class with some concrete direction to take the story, a direction that she herself states.

Advice, part 2:

- As a last note of empathy: it is natural to feel defensive during workshop. Sometimes it is hard to know when to listen and when to redirect. During the description, listen and absorb the interpretations of your work. Later you can help guide the discussion toward your biggest concerns. Please do jump in if you feel as if the workshop is completely misinterpreting, but maybe first ask why. You will never have a more engaged audience than people who must read and comment on your work.
- When you are workshopped, it is important to remember that you will not connect with

everything that is said. You shouldn't! Don't listen to everything; *don't take every suggestion—* trust your instincts. Think hard, though, about all the questions asked of you. Are you making your decisions consciously enough? Are there decisions you made subconsciously that turned out to be even better (or worse) than you expected? Don't ever try to make your story into someone else's story, or especially the group's story. That will ruin what you love about your story and so will ruin your story. Part of being in a writing community is learning who is a good reader for your work, and how to incorporate suggestions into your own intentions and process. Also remember that while you might not like a suggestion, the most important thing about a critique might be simply its existence. The point remains that that part of your story might have tripped up this group of test readers, and if they are reading carefully, you can use that knowledge to find your own solution or even your own problem. Also remember that sometimes making a certain part of a story work isn't about that part of the story, but about an earlier part, or a later part, or the whole thing, or the basic foundation. What is most important is to know that there's still work to do and to be inspired to do it.

- Don't come into workshop wanting to hear your story is perfect. That's what publication is for.
- Being workshopped can be emotionally exhausting, but know that the feeling will pass. Be empathetic toward others. They are feeling the same way or maybe even worse. Remember always that the workshop is meant to spur the author to keep working on the story, not abandon it. Encouraging further writing should always be our goal.
- It can be best to take a week or longer, after your workshop, before reading through and evaluating the comments on your story. Sometimes it takes quite a while to be able to "listen" to what you've heard.
- Some encouragement (hopefully)! The bulk of successful writing is in the fact that you have an endless number of tries. Persistence is key.

3. Banned from Workshop

These phrases and/or variants should not be used in workshop. (We'll discuss reasons why.)

Related to evaluation
> Plausible/not plausible/this wouldn't happen in real life, etc.

X character wouldn't/would do this
Buy it/earned/pay off/etc.—the
    evaluation of fiction here will not be
    capitalist
Fiction can't/has to
Unlikeable/likeable/relatable/etc.
"Show, don't tell"
"Melodramatic" unless used to refer
    to the specific literary tradition of
    melodrama

Related to workshop etiquette
    "The author"—the author is a real
        person in the room, one of the key
        advantages to workshop
    You should/you shouldn't/you need to/
        etc.

Related to audience (e.g. you are not *the* reader of
the story):
    "*The* reader"
    I want/I need/I'd like/I feel/I find/etc.
    I relate
    This reminds me of when I . . .

As a counterbalance, here are some helpful ways of framing comments (notice the questions):

What would the story be like if . . .

How would the story change if . . .

What do you think about . . . / Have you thought
about . . .

I noticed (on page X) . . .

The first time I read the story . . . vs. the second
time I read the story . . .

This reminds me of the story X . . . (less but sometimes helpful are other media like film, TV,
painting, etc.)

4. A List of Craft Questions to Take into Consideration
Here are a few items to investigate while reading your
peers' and your own work. Ask yourself these questions,
then address them where appropriate. Note that this list
is just to get you started, that it is by no means exhaustive,
and that our definitions will change as we go. There is
much more that could and should be considered.

- **Action**: What happens? What is the reason it
  happens? Is it linked causally? Is what happens
  satisfying? Does it work thematically? Does it
  reveal character? Is anything happening? Is
  enough happening? Is too much happening?
  How do you make sense of the various actions
  together? What do the actions mean?
- **Agency**: Who causes the action? Whose

decisions move the plot forward? Whose desires? Does the main character have the most agency? Or are there other forces that have more agency? Why is the protagonist the protagonist? How does agency work in the world—who has it and who doesn't? Why? How do the characters show their agency? How do they use it or give it up? How can they have more agency? What does the amount of agency the characters have say about their position in society? About an aesthetic sensibility? About theme?

- **Arc**: How does the protagonist change (or try hard to change and fail)? (Character arc) How does the world change or fail to change? (Story arc) Are these arcs satisfying/resonant? Do they work together? What do they mean about the characters, the world, the theme, the purpose of the story, the audience?

- **Audience**: For whom/to whom is this piece written, ideally? How can you tell? How does it affect the writing? What expectations are being assumed? Met? Undermined? Disregarded? What tradition does the work fall into? What kind of publication would this be published in? Is there a regional audience? Gendered? Raced? What is explicit and what is implicit? What would more or clearer focus on audience mean for the story? What would it look like?

- **Characterization**: Does the audience have a clear vision of who the characters are? What makes a character different from any other? Are they described via physical details, age, gender, locale, socioeconomic status, race, sexuality? What is left out and why? What does characterization say about theme, purpose, audience? Do we know the characters' wants and fears? Toward each other? Toward themselves? Toward the world? Is it clear where they work? Live? Do they have families, friends, lovers, enemies, frenemies? How much does the audience need to know to understand the characters' particular identity positions in the world? Are the characters shown through *decision* and *action*? Otherwise? Why? What is their attitude in a given situation? In general?

- **Conflict**: What is standing in the way of the protagonist (and other characters) getting what they want? Does this conflict escalate/ complicate as the story progresses? Does the story let the characters off the hook? Why? Does this conflict come from outside and inside? Is this a story that leans toward fate or toward free will? Do the various conflicts work together thematically? If there is no conflict, what does the work of conflict in the story? What changes how things are desired or how those desires are understood?

- **Context**: What information does the story need to present in order to make sense *to its audience*? Does the story present too much information for its audience? Too little? In the right places? What larger context does the story engage with? What larger context does it disregard or assume? Does the material give the appropriate information to make sense of where things are in the story/on the page? Do we get information too early? Too late? How does the story convey information? How could it convey information more efficiently?

- **Grounding**: What clues does the story give to its audience to situate the story in time and space? Do we know what is happening? Who the characters are? What the premise is? When time is passing? How much time has passed? Should we know these things, if we are or are not the audience?

- **Inside/Outside Story**: Is there an inside and outside story going on—i.e. is there an internal change happening vs. an external change happening? Is there action and change both outside of the protagonist and within her/him? For example, the protagonist chickens out, his wife has an affair, the protagonist faces a lion vs. the protagonist feels himself come alive and change for a brief instant into the man he wants to be ("The Short Happy Life of Francis Macomber"). The first is the outside story, the second the inside story.

- **Language**: How is the language being used appropriate to the story, situation, characters, etc.? Syntax, diction? For the audience? What does it reveal about characters, audience, theme, world? Where does it seem to pick up in energy? Where does it seem to lose energy? Why? What sounds does it traffic in? What rhythms/meters?

- **Pacing**: What is the balance of summary and scene? Does backstory slow the story down or help deepen the stakes? How much time do we spend with the most significant characters and actions of the story? How much do we spend on less central things (to the audience)? What can be cut? What should be added? How does the author's "breath" change throughout the story?

- **Perspective/Point of View**: Is the point of view clear and consistent? What does the POV choice mean thematically? Aesthetically? Does form match content? Is the psychic distance appropriate? Too far? Too close? Not enough variety/movement? Whose story is it? Would first or third person (or even second) work better? Why?

- **Raison d'Être**: Why this story on this particular day, at this particular time, in this particular place? Is this the *most important* moment in this character's life? Is this the right moment to tell the story? What is going on at the point of telling?

- **Setting**: How does the setting affect the story? How does it factor into what happens and who people are? Why this setting and no other? Does the setting appear on the page both explicitly and implicitly? Does it affect the inside and outside story? How aware of the setting are the characters? Is the narrator? Is the story? How aware of the real world is the story?

- **Stakes**: Is it clear what stands to be gained or lost during the events of the story? In the telling of the story? Between the story and the world? Are the stakes high enough in each case? Are they different for different characters, for different audiences? Does the protagonist care what happens? Why? How? What are the story's objective stakes? What are the story's subjective stakes? Do the story stakes rise as the story progresses?

- **Structure**: Do the passages of the story appear

in the most meaningful order? What is the meaning? Is it different for different audiences? Do early sections of the story foreshadow later parts? Should they? Are transitions effective? Are all scenes "doing something" to advance the story in the order that they are in? What is the audience expected to remember from earlier in the story? What is the audience expected to forget? How is the story organized and how does that help accomplish (or not) the story's effect? How does form represent/do justice to content? How would the story be different if it were organized differently? What does the structure say about how we make meaning in the world?

- **Tone**: How is the story oriented toward the world? The narrator? The characters? Is the story supposed to be funny? Dark? Melodramatic? Campy? Etc. Does it depend on the audience? Why? What in the story gives you this feeling? How does the story convey its tone? Through what other elements? Setting? Style? Stakes? Characterization? Voice?

- **Voice**: How is the story told? How much is narrative summary? What is in narrative summary and why? Are there parentheticals? Italics? Where is the emphasis? Why? How old is the narrator or point-of-view character?

How educated? Cultural background? Formal? Informal? What makes this voice different from any other? Why this voice and not another? What is shown and what is told? Why? What are the metaphors used and how do they create a sense of voice? How much detail comes into play and what kind of detail? Who is telling the story? Why? How do you know? How are they addressing an implicit or explicit listener?

- **Vulnerability**: What does the story risk? How is the story the author's and the author's alone? Does the story challenge the status quo? Does it challenge its characters enough? Does it challenge its author? What is still in hiding?

- **Beginning**: Does the beginning introduce us to characters and situation and stakes effectively? Does it set up our expectations for the rest of the story? Does it teach us the rules of the story? Is it extraneous? Does it explain too much/not enough? Where does it suggest the story might go? How does it establish audience? How does it encourage its audience to keep reading? What does it "promise" its audience? What does it "demand" from them?

- **Ending**: Does the ending fulfill or undermine expectations set earlier in the story? How so? Or how not? What does this mean? Are the audience's questions answered or addressed or purposely and satisfyingly left unanswered? Should more happen? Less? Would the answer be the same for the ideal audience? Does the ending explain too much/not enough for that audience? How has it delivered on or subverted the expectations the story set up in the beginning? What does it mean to read the story teleologically/what does the ending mean to how we make meaning of the action in the whole? What does the ending tell us about what a story is and does?

WORKSHOPPING INCOMPLETE DRAFTS

I used to believe a writer should submit to workshop only a draft she had taken as far as she could take on her own, since, as a student, I had watched so many workshops simply reflect back to the writer what she already knew. The workshop became about confirmation, rather than opportunity. But my teaching reality means often workshopping writers' early drafts and knowing it is up to the instructor to make these workshops as helpful as they can be. This task is impossible in silence. If the writer is gagged, the workshop wastes valuable time identifying what the writer can identify for herself. Instead, the writer that identifies her story's weaknesses and goals for the workshop is able to make her concerns the context of the discussion, rather than its puzzle. In other words, both later and earlier drafts, and even *partial* drafts, can benefit a lot from workshop—so long as the workshop is not one-size-fits-all.

Indeed the workshop's difficulty with partial drafts is the workshop's difficulty with centering the author (see the chapter "Who Is at the Center of Workshop and Who Should Be?"). Its focus is not actually on process but on product. Despite its many claims to be about process, the traditional model is always discussing what a story may eventually become rather than its becoming. Only a product needs to be interpreted from the page alone.

Here is an example. In a smaller workshop, I often let students turn in a lot of work at once, especially when they're interested in writing novels. In one such class, all but one student turned in at least seventy pages. The final student, however, turned in four very rough pages without giving us much context to understand what she had written. If she had stayed silent in workshop and we had talked about what we knew from those four pages alone, her workshop would have been a complete failure. We had to do something different.

Novel workshops almost always address partial drafts, early drafts. In my experience, an early novel draft looks nothing like its published form. What would be the point of these workshops looking only at the existing pages? Why would the author need to be there at all? She could simply listen to a recording. Novel workshops are most effective when they treat the manuscript as only a glimpse into the author's next five to ten years of process—again, as context and not as content. In order to do this, the workshop needs to know what the author's *process* looks like.

When we workshopped my student's four pages, we started by asking her what she would do next, assuming she wasn't going to go back and edit those four pages over and over again. If she had said she would write whatever the next scene was, we would have taken her workshop from there, but she wanted to do more planning. She told us about everything she knew so far, what difficulties she anticipated, what she loved about the idea, and what we could help with. We talked about where the four pages we had read might fit into her larger idea, and what some possible shapes of such a novel might look like. She talked about novels she liked and how they might make useful models. Then we made a list of the questions that had come up during the discussion, making a distinction between which questions were usefully mysterious for now and which questions might be answered in a way that might create *more* mystery. At the end of the workshop, I asked again what the student would do next, and she had a much more concrete idea of where she was going.

I have my students do self-reflections on their workshops. They write about what helped and what didn't help, what suggestions were useful, what questions they still have, etc. Then we meet to discuss both their workshop and their work. This particular student wrote that she had gone into workshop full of dread, expecting her prose to be ripped apart, because that was what she had been taught to expect, and instead, for the first time, she felt inspired to write more. I always tell my students that this is our goal, for the writer to leave workshop wanting to go back to work. Wanting to reengage with process, rather than feeling intimidated by product.

To ask the writer to submit work that is further along, or to require her to submit a full draft, means in many cases that the writer will face the same kind of arbitrary deadlines she faces in the rest of her work life. Some people do better with deadlines. For others, the creative process may be less deadline-oriented and preferably so. Some writers have the privilege to write every day. Others write when they can. Some writers start at the beginning. Others jump around. Just because a manuscript includes a beginning, middle, and end, in that order, doesn't mean it results in a better workshop. It results in a product that the workshop can more easily evaluate as a product. Process is what the writer will carry with her after any single story or workshop is done.

AGAINST PAGE LIMITS

As a student I was lucky to mostly avoid page limits on workshop manuscripts. When we asked Margot Livesey how many pages to submit, she would say, "whatever is right for the story." "Whatever is right for the story" was, in fact, a frequent topic in workshop. I took it to mean that a story's length is to be defined by the project and not by an arbitrary limit, even the limit of its author. Over the years I either stole or made up a phrase to describe this (Google suggests that I made it up). I tell students to ask of their work and others': "Does the length match the reach?"

I say the same thing when students ask how long individual scenes should be. Instead of a length, I will offer a list of things I like my scenes to do—such as shift the character and the plot, include symbolic action, start in one emotional or physical or intellectual place and end in another (standard scene-fare)—and suggest that their scenes go as short or as long as they need to go in order to accomplish their own goals.

In fact, I was naive enough to think length

requirements had gone out of fashion, so when a friend asked how many pages she should tell her students to submit, I was alone in answering "whatever is right for the story." I was surprised to see other writers offer concrete suggestions: eight to ten pages or ten to fifteen.

I never sit down to write an eight-to-ten-page or ten-to-fifteen-page story. Never. An eight-to-ten-page story is the result of realizing at some point that a story will need about eight to ten pages to accomplish its goals. Instead of *how long something should be*, in other words, one might ask *what a thing is*. What is a scene? Is it a thing this many sentences long or something else? What is a story? Is it a thing this many pages long or something else?

The reason for length limits in workshop must be time. So why not require a time limit instead? When my students ask how long a manuscript should be, I ask them how long we should take with each workshop packet— one hour, or two—and we set a fixed amount of time. This means that a student who turns in a one-paragraph story receives the same amount of reading and commenting time as a student who turns in a thirty-page story. The first student might receive quite a lot of comments and questions, quite a lot of line-editing, quite a long note on her one-paragraph story, and the second student might get broader comments and no line-edits while still the same attentiveness. Likely the difference would actually serve the stories: the one-paragraph story might rely more on the line than a thirty-page story anyway.

If a time limit necessitates more explanation than a page limit, I also talk about and include in the syllabus language about how to read and comment on fiction for workshop, i.e. how to spend that time. In my experience, this specificity has always alleviated student concerns about "fairness." Allocating time is a simple solution to the length question with its own measure of equality. But lastly let's look at four more problems with assigning a length requirement.

1. Writers often have a certain length they are drawn to (see the section on pacing). An obvious example is that some writers write only novels and others only short stories; still others only flash fiction. Length limits often force bloated or barely drawn prose. A ten-page limit means that a writer who needs twenty pages might try to squeeze her twenty in.

2. Most writers need both limits and freedom. So we should be careful where we encourage these limits and freedom. Length may not be the most useful limit.

3. Eight to ten pages, intentionally or not, encourages students to think eight to ten pages is best. Especially for a beginning writer, to say, "Turn into workshop a story of eight to ten pages," is to say: "To your professor (whose authority you put some degree of trust in) a

good length for a story is eight to ten pages."
Internalize this and it becomes: "A good story
is eight to ten pages." At best, that kind of
implicit message requires a lot of unteaching,
and do we want to spend the time we have to
unteach on unteaching the things that we
ourselves taught?

4. This is how you get chapters and/or stories
all of the same length (and sometimes pacing and arc and even structure, etc.). Because
requiring writers to write to certain expectations primes them to write to certain expectations (and audiences).

FOUR THINGS TO GRADE

For writers teaching in academia, a common question is how to grade student writing. No one seems much to like grading fiction for quality. It's not very objective and doesn't seem to improve the writing. So what else is there? I have seen various grading strategies, mostly to do with grading some form of participation. I offer here four other options:

1. The Critique Letter as a Form

I grade and comment on critique letters in order to get students thinking about them as a form. I give extensive guidelines for what I am looking for, and we talk in class about what is helpful in letters. Early in the course, I make a lot of comments to try to correct students' tendencies to center themselves in their critique of the writer, to ask more questions and more open-ended questions, to frame their suggestions as what-ifs rather than as criticism or prescription, etc. I don't try to shape their fiction, but I do think it helps with letters. Students know how to write to a form (which is another reason workshop can be so dangerously persuasive), and with guidance, their letters become more complex, less self-centered, less didactic, more questioning, more specific, etc. Students are more prepared for workshop and come to share a language of critique, which increases their comfort with the letters they write and the letters they receive from their peers.

2. *Workshop Self-Reflections*

When students reflect on how their workshops were and were not particularly helpful, they also reflect on their manuscript and what they can immediately apply from workshop, what revision might look like. They process and synthesize the workshop comments and also process their feelings about those comments. These reflections also help them to become better workshoppers, as they identify what they themselves found useful from the author's seat. Additionally, these reflections can guide student-teacher conferences (I meet with students once they have processed the workshop and are ready to talk about what comes next). Knowing a student's thoughts about her workshop helps conferences start on more shared ground. The instructor can then directly address any lingering questions the student might have, and some students find it easier to write down concerns they may be too shy to bring up in person.

3. Revision, Before and After

In order to encourage students to get invested in revision, they can do a "revision plan" that lists some of the things they might try out. Pre-thinking/prediction is useful. The plans help them visualize the process. After they try any specific strategy, they should reflect on how it went, in what ways it was useful and in what ways it was not, how they deviated from their plans, how their plans might change now, how their understanding of their stories might have changed. Again, as they write about the revision process, they will come to a better understanding of it and of the way they themselves work. Reading a student's predictions and results also allows the instructor more objective insight into the writer's process.

4. Self-Analysis of Elements of Fiction

"Self-Analysis of Elements of Fiction" is what I call an assignment in which students clarify their cultural aesthetics using the craft language we have used in class. They write about how plot, arc, stakes, characterization, etc., operate in their own work—which traditions and genres they are working within, what other fiction they might be using as models or influence, how their working definitions of these terms relate to class discussions, etc. The assignment both asks them to think critically about how they are working with and contributing to culture, and gives me a chance to see their engagement with the information from lectures and discussion. All of this contributes to a more conscious and culturally conscious use of and conversation about craft.

APPENDIX: EXERCISES

PURPOSE-ORIENTED WRITING EXERCISES

For vulnerability/introductions:
1. List three moments in which you felt like you were not yourself.
2. Instructor distributes lists randomly among the class. (If a student gets her own list, she should immediately exchange it.)
3. Write a story using at least two of the three items on the list you got. Consider how to get onto the page the kind of investment and vulnerability that your classmate shared, even though you personally have no connection to these moments.

First-page exercise:
1. Share and read the first page of a new or newly in-progress story, in a group of three.

2. The two readers should . . .
   a. describe the story (including the audience)
   b. say where they think it is going
   c. name what is most interesting so far.
3. Rewrite your opening without looking at the old first page.

For audience (adapted from a workshop with Mat Johnson):

1. Name the one person or few people who first see your work/to whom you're writing and who would get every reference—e.g., my best friend from grad school.
2. Describe an audience of about one thousand who would be ideal readers for your book/whom you hope to reach—e.g., college-graduate male Korean American adoptees politically active between thirty and forty, in a heterosexual relationship, with kids, who read more than twenty books a year.
3. Describe an audience of about twenty thousand who would make your book a bestseller—e.g., college graduate Asian Americans between thirty and forty, with kids, who are politically active and read more than twenty books a year.
4. Now, write. Write a paragraph about your protagonist's identity that accommodates an

outside audience. Rewrite that paragraph to address your specific readers. How is it different?

For plot and consequences:

1. In five minutes, write as many sentences as you can that follow this format:
    If s/h/t hadn't _____, _____ wouldn't have _____.

    (For example: "If she hadn't tried to cross the road, her boyfriend's car wouldn't have flipped over.")

2. Expand one of the sentences into a paragraph, including a full set of actions and character(s).

3. Expand the paragraph into a scene.

For characterization (adapted from Danzy Senna):

In five minutes, write as many sentences as you can about the same character using the following construction:

S/h/t was the type of person who _____.

(E.g. "She was the type of person who went to the bowling alley every Friday, but never bowled.")

Push past the obvious and easy. If it's still easy after five minutes, go for ten.

For point of view:

1. Write a scene about something minor that happened to you (personally) this week, but

in third-person POV. (For example, going to the grocery store and buying oranges.) Create a character to fit the scene/fictionalize. Don't choose anything too obviously important, just a passing moment.

2. Now move your story ten years into the future. The minor action from your scene has turned out to be extremely momentous—it has changed your character's life. Write about that moment from the perspective of the character ten years into the future, looking back with a sense of how momentous the moment turned out to be. Do this in first person. Don't forget to include how the world has changed.

For voice:

1. List your fears, both past and present. (Not something triggering, something irrational. For example, I have a fear of dolls.)

2. Write a fictional scene in which one of those fears plays out: a doll comes to life and just wants love, but creepily. Write in the voice of the person experiencing fear. How does what happens affect and change how your character sees the world?

3. Write the same scene from the voice of someone causing fear. Or perhaps from the voice of

a non-active witness. Compare word choices, psychic distance, etc.

For structure:

Write a structural metaphor for your story—e.g. the dolphin that surfaces beside the boat as a structural metaphor for the way the story keeps skimming along the surface/dipping into the past. Or, a more cliché example, a tree in a family's backyard in a story that branches into several different family members' perspectives.

For prolepsis (flash-forwards) and true/false mystery (mystery shared by the characters vs. mystery only for the readers, e.g. whodunit in a first-person detective novel):

Write a one-page story that starts with the sentence "By the end of this story, character X and character Y will fall in love and, in so doing, character X will murder character Y." How does revealing everything up front change how the story operates? Does it imply one audience vs. another?

Now try writing the story without revealing what will happen until the moment it happens. What are the differences?

For tone:

Write a scene with a pessimistic protagonist, but in an optimistic tone. Or write a scene with an optimist in a pessimistic tone. In other words, the protagonist's orientation toward the world should be the opposite of the story's orientation toward the world. Go back and identify what strategies you used to establish tone, both consciously and unconsciously: e.g. diction, plot, characterization, setting, etc.

For objects:

Write a scene with two objects in play, one on display and one hidden. By the end of the scene, hide the object that was on display and reveal the object that was hidden.

For context:

1. Describe a place that is in some way emotionally charged for your protagonist. Make sure you include both descriptive context and dramatic context: what makes the place charged for this particular character?

2. Someone there is different from everyone else—describe that person, again both with descriptive context and dramatic context: what makes the person stand out?

3. That person has a mysterious box—describe the box. If there is dramatic context, note that it has moved completely to the character's imagination.

4. The person makes a request of the protagonist

and hands over the box. Now finish the story, using the context you have set up.

(This order of giving context mirrors the way a movie might start with a wide shot and then zoom in. You are going from world to character to the collision between them.)

34 REVISION EXERCISES

1.

The first exercise here is more like advice. For me, the most important question in revision is "Am I bored here?" The hardest and most useful truth about writing that I was ever told is that when I get bored reading my own writing, it's not because I have read it so many times, it's because it is boring. Writers tell themselves all sorts of excuses—one common excuse is that what we find boring in our own work would be interesting to someone else if she was reading it for the first time. Don't believe it. Even if you read over your story a thousand times, you will always be the most invested in it, because it is yours. Excite yourself. If something interests you, you can work with it. If it bores you, it is simply boring.

2.

Read your work aloud to yourself or a friend. You will hear things that ring false; you will improve your sense of what has sonic impact; you will learn your own aesthetic values. Now change the font, the margins, the text color, and record yourself reading. Then play it back and listen as if you are the friend. You want to see your work both from your own perspective and someone else's. Eventually you can be your own workshop, your own ideal reader.

3.

Do this: Make a map of your story. Get some blank sheets of paper, one for every three pages of your manuscript. Split each sheet into three columns. Each column represents a page. Now draw lines across each column where the story seems to break. Decide for yourself where these breaks may be. Many might be space breaks in the story; others might be breaks between characters, between timelines, between narrative summary and scene, etc. Then, in each individual section you've created:

    a.   Write down any action that happens in that section.

    b.   Write down what work each section does for the story. What is its purpose(s)? To raise the stakes? To complicate a relationship? To move the plot? Etc.

    c.   Write down any themes that show up in each section.

    d.   Shade the sections that happen in the past.

    e.   Note any characters who show up.

    f.   Note any settings.

    g.   Write down any desires in play and anything

that complicates or stands in the way of those desires.

You can use this map to help you with the other prompts below. You might want to cut your story up along the same lines and tape it to the wall. Once you have "re-envisioned" your manuscript in this way, rearrange it so that only two or three "sections" that you have identified remain in the same spot. Every other section should be moved. If that means you have to add or delete scenes, do so. Do whatever you need to do to make your story work again. Now regroup, rethink.

4.

Answer for yourself the following foundational questions:

- Whom are you writing for?
- What is the story about?
- What is the central complication?
- What are the stakes?
- What does the protagonist want?
- How is the protagonist's world different from any other character's?
- How does the protagonist eventually change or fail to change? How does the world change or fail to be changed?
- Where are the gaps where something could be added? What is missing?
- What is extraneous?

5.

List every decision your protagonist makes, in the order they appear in the story, everything from what she wears or eats to how she reacts to or makes trouble. Now either change the order of the decisions your protagonist makes so that they follow a causal chain OR figure out what outside force is causing a lot of the decisions and build out the list of effects. When you have a new list, rearrange your story to reflect it. Play around. Have fun. Cut at least one major decision and/or action, with (if this applies) the corresponding scene. Change the chronology—many stories are not in chronological order, but move around via flashbacks, memories, flash-forwards, imagined scenes, etc.

6.

Create a list of decisions for other major characters. Ask yourself: Who makes the most decisions in the story, implicitly or explicitly? Whose decisions have the most impact on the world? Do you want the protagonist to make more decisions? To have more agency? Try to identify how each character's decisions impact the other characters.

Related: What cultural influences inform the characters' decisions?

Related: What does the character want: _____

What stops the character from getting it: _____

What makes it easier: _____

Really examine what goes in the third blank. Authorial choices about what makes the world easier or harder are choices about privilege, agency, political beliefs, etc.

7.

Using sticky notes, track what your readers learn on each page. (You could do this once for your ideal audience and once for an unlikely audience.) Use different-color sticky notes for different kinds of information—information about characters, about setting, about plot, about stakes, etc. Where does the manuscript start to give more or less information? For example: at a certain point, the purpose of a character's actions change from new information to playing out or contradicting what we already know. As you look at the arrangement of sticky notes, watch out for information dumps. Remember to modulate: how does information "tune" a story to its audience and how does a story keep its audience surprised?

8.

Mark each spot a new character enters a story, and write an extended introduction for that character, including what they look like, how they are dressed, what objects are associated with them, any identifying marks, any identifying habits or gestures, their way of seeing things, their attitude toward the world, their age, their ethnicity, their occupation, their family relationships and history, their relationship to the protagonist, another character's opinion of them, their desires, their problems, their faults, etc. Character description usually comes as soon as we meet a character because we are used to first impressions and because we are taught to accept more information at first than later on. (This cultural expectation is not obvious—I was once in a workshop where a writer asked why Michael Chabon kept describing his characters as soon as they came up, why he didn't save some for later.) In the extended introduction, also include at least one paragraph of backstory: what do you know about their pasts, how they've come to be who they are now or how different they are now from before?

When you are done introducing the characters, find where each major character last shows up in the manuscript. Now add extended descriptions of them in their final appearances: Have they changed at all within the story? Do they look different, act different, etc., from earlier? How has their position in the world affected them or kept them from being affected? How have they changed the world or failed to change it? Could they change more? Should they? Have we seen these changes in action?

Once you've written these intros and outros for your characters, cut most of them. Cut what you don't need or move it elsewhere in the story, and keep what you need. Keep what "gets the character in the door": what makes them different from everyone else, what makes them a "kind of person." Is it that your character stays up until everyone else has gone to bed and waits for the neighborhood stray to poke its head into the yard, but then never goes out to talk to it or pet it, just looks at it longingly? Etc. Track each character through the story. How does the new information you know about the character affect their actions and behavior, and the story's overall tone, stakes, plot, etc.?

9.

At the end of your story, skip forward in time at least ten years and write at least one more scene. In that scene, the protagonist acts and/or narrates with an awareness of all the dramatic consequences from the events of ten years earlier. How are they different now? See if you can put this scene into the story someplace (not necessarily at the end). How is the story different now? Do what you can to fulfill the new possibilities.

10.

Add a major source of outside complication to your story. That is, add something big that comes in and forces itself on the plot, something like a toxic spill or an earthquake or a war or a rabid dog or a serial killer or a rapture. Don't make this a small insertion, but something that truly changes the story. You might think about what large outside force would connect thematically to the character arc. In other words, how can story arc and character arc inform each other and help each other to resonate? A toxic spill (and subsequent cover-up) might help a story in

which a character is hiding a secret that would reveal him
to be a dangerous person.

11.

What are the other possibilities for your story? Underline
all the "missed opportunities" in your manuscript. Or,
better yet, have a friend or your writing partner (someone in your ideal audience) do this for you. Add as much
as you can for *every single* missed opportunity. Now cut at
least half of what you've added. Rearrange the story and
do whatever you need to do to make the story work again.

12.

Identify the "symbolic action" in each scene—what happens that represents the shift in a character's emotions
or growth, in the situation or world (even if these shifts
are slight). Add symbolic action where you are missing
it. Does the character who has just found out her family
has gone bankrupt suddenly spill her drink all over her
clothes in shock? Does the character who learns to be a
better person help the same homeless person she ignored
at the beginning of the story? Try to get the most significant symbolic action close to the end of the scene. Try to
give your protagonist more symbolic action in general.

13.

Highlight anything that is backstory (this could be entire
flashbacks or single sentences or parts of sentences). Cut

the manuscript up, page by page, with scissors, so that you've cut out everything that happens in the story's past. Tape the cut-up sections to the wall, starting a new column with each page. Tape what is present on the top and what is past on the bottom.

What does the balance between past and present look like? For the backstory you cut out, identify whether each piece is absolutely necessary. Then ask yourself *where* it is absolutely necessary—for one, ask yourself where it would put the most pressure on the present. Remember that going into the past inherently delays the story's present, so especially for an audience that values the present, backstory should be used to increase urgency in the present time. For example, if you have a character encountering her mother on page 15, where is the backstory about the mother that makes that encounter harrowing? On page 3? On page 20? Why not on page 14 or 15 or 16? Is there a clear reason we go into the past when we do and a clear reason to come back to the present? What are those reasons?

Delete as much of the past as you can (whatever isn't necessary). Try to put as much of the necessary backstory as you can into the present instead. Think about what information is being conveyed. Can you put the backstory in dialogue? Can you get the same information across through action? Attitude? Implication?

Finally, interrogate the story past on a sentence level. For example, a sentence like "<u>The fishermen had just finished dragging in their nets</u> and were going to get a drink" could be "The fisherman finished dragging in their nets and went for a drink." More action in the present of the story, even on that small a level, can make the story feel more active.

14.

Utilize objects. Try to get objects into each scene and associate each character with an object. To be reminded of a birthmark or always unmatching socks or the hat a character never takes off can bring to mind the entire picture we first got of them. Objects can also remind us of various characters' subplots or can be used to reinforce theme. Use recurring objects, objects that appear earlier in your story and reappear later, either in their same form or transformed. Make at least one object "track" through the story, appearing at multiple points and signaling differences from the last point, either through how the characters interact with the object, or how they feel about it, or what it looks like, how it has changed, etc. When you have filled the story with objects, cut the ones that don't seem to add meaning. Keep in mind that what we think about objects and even what we think of *as* objects is cultural and influences theme. Are non-human animals objects or subjects? What about the land? Or the weather?

15.

Get rid of one character or more. Kill them off or simply erase them. Or fuse characters together to make a single character. How does their removal change the world of the story? Characters exist in relation to each other—this is why we can understand who they are by understanding how they are different. What is missing now? What are the positionalities of the characters who are left? If you need another character again, make one up instead of returning to one you cut.

16.

The world acts. Make sure setting has an effect on the story and is not just a place to set it, a stage for the characters to act on. Try this: consolidate your settings to one to three total. If each setting has more room on the page now, how can setting be more involved in the story, how can it change and be changed by the characters? Expand until the story is the same length as before, with fewer settings doing more work.

17.

If your story is in first-person POV, write a scene (not just summary) from the narrator's point of telling. Narrators are always telling a story from a future point, even in present tense—an implied future point just after the action or a future point far later. What is your narrator doing with her life when she is telling this story? Where is she? Who is she now? What is her world like? What does she know now about the world? What does she know at that future point that is different from what she knew during the present of the story's action? You may need to bring in another character. Make sure you're depicting not only the narrator but also the world. If the world is exactly the same as it was earlier, why?

18.

Start by underlining (or however you want to do it) anything that moves the character arc/inside story forward (thoughts, emotions, etc.). Then over-line (draw a line over the top of, or highlight, or however you want to do it) anything that moves the story arc/outside story forward. Look for places where the inside story and outside story overlap. Look for places where the inside story could be heightened and add things there about the character arc. Look for places where there could be more outside story and add some action.

Most of all: look for (a) places where the inside story affects, or should affect and does not yet affect, the outside story (emotions that lead to action or so forth) and (b) places where the outside story affects, or should affect and does not yet affect, the inside story (action leads to emotion or so forth). Try to create causation between the inside and outside story so that the two are intricately linked.

Make sure both inside and outside story have an arc. What kind of arc? What expectations are you working with or against? How do the two arcs create meaning between them?

19.

Write past your ending. Write one or two or more scenes after the end of your story. Even if these scenes don't make it into the final version, they will help inform it. What happens right after the end of your story? And don't stop there: now write about what the consequences are of what happens, and whether your characters accept or reject those consequences.

20.

Add a scene with a character who arrives for only that one scene and interacts with your protagonist. (This should be a character from the world outside the plot—a character your protagonist has not already been thinking of as part of the story's situation. An example would be a prank phone call or an old friend coming to town.) How does the protagonist's understanding of the world change? How does the audience's understanding change? Does the outside character help the protagonist put things in "perspective," or does the interaction blow things up even more?

21.

Write one anchor scene with all of your main characters in the same room, maybe even talking. What is the setting, how do they interact with each other, how do they relate to each other, etc.? Do they experience the world similarly or differently? Do they occupy the same spaces regularly? How do their positions in the world cause conflict or complications? Introduce everyone within one scene and then work off of that scene. Maybe you already have that scene and you reorganize your story to center it, or maybe you add that scene.

22.

Add a scene that changes the context in which we know the characters—maybe they go on a trip, or maybe they are always together but now we see them apart, or maybe someone important to them comes to visit and they have to be on their best behavior, or maybe they go to a party full of people of a different race or full of people of the same race, etc.

23.

Especially when they do not have an ideal audience in mind, writers tend to explain more than is necessary or compelling. Try this: Cut the opening paragraph of the story. Cut the last paragraph. (If you are brave, do this for each scene or chapter.) When I edited fiction, this was the edit I asked for most often. Reread the story—does it *need* what was cut? Rewrite what your audience really must know, but don't just add it back in; write it better.

24.

In each paragraph, look at the opening sentence and last sentence in particular. It is important what goes where.

We are taught in American schools to read as if the most important information is at the beginning and end of a paragraph, the beginning and end of a section, the beginning and end of an essay or story or so forth. Skimming, on tests, is done in the middle. You can use this to your advantage. Things that will come back later in the story can be hidden in the middle (at least for a Western audience). Important things in the moment can be emphasized if you include them at the beginning or end. A good last line is a good last line, but might only make an okay middle line.

25.

Make a list of all the plot points in your story. Your protagonist needs to reckon with them. Box or underline the plot points that present a change from your character's norms or routine. How is normal changing? For the protagonist? For the world? You are identifying reasons why you're telling the story NOW, the story of this day/event(s), which is generally an important component of plot (raison d'être).

You might think of the basic fairy tale structure:

> Once upon a time
> Every day
> <u>One day</u>
> <u>And then</u>
> <u>And then</u>

And then

Etc.

Happily ever after

Underlined are the plot points unique to the NOW of the story. The fairy tale structure sets up character and setting and routine, then has something break that routine that sets off a plot full of action that has never happened before. Many plots work like this, because what happened before is the status quo, and plot is about what breaks the status quo forever (and institutes a new, better or worse status quo) or how the status quo reasserts itself. We expect a story to be what happens when things are *not* normal.

Try reordering or rearranging the story in this fairy tale format, starting with the norms and then getting to the "one day"—to the changes—that make the rest of the story about acceptance or rejection of consequences up to or until the very end. Either disguise the fairy tale structure so that it does not become a focus of the story, or write for an audience who would recognize the fairy tale structure and enjoy the recognition.

26.

Go through your story and underline anything abstract, such as ideas, emotions, vague bits, etc. Now go back and try to replace everything you've underlined with a more concrete way of expressing the same thing. For example: "Tori missed having someone to kiss" might become "Tori climbed up onto her roof with her binoculars and found the X she had marked where she had had her first kiss in her childhood tree house." Or, you know, something better than that. If you are writing for an audience who loves abstraction, try adding something concrete beforehand. For example the sentence about the tree house might be followed by a couple of sentences about how Tori's fear of heights is now attached to her feelings of love: "Her legs had trembled as she descended from that first kiss. Ever since that day, she had been confused about whether she was afraid of heights or of love." Or, you know, something better than that.

27.

List all the context in your story. Separate it into "descriptive context" and "dramatic context." I'm adapting these terms from Robert Boswell: descriptive context (what Boswell calls "general context") is used for grounding and world-building (setting, age, time period, etc.) and dramatic context is used for establishing what makes something dramatic (usually something personal to the character and the character's desires, stakes, arc, and so forth). For example, you might imagine running into two different people from high school. The descriptive context can be more or less the same: where the characters are, how old they are, their jobs and sociocultural position, etc. But one might be an ex-boyfriend and one might be just a forgotten classmate. The dramatic context is different.

After you've made your list, figure out where best to put all that context. Ask, especially, what exactly the dramatic context is making more dramatic, and make sure the context is beside the drama. As with backstory, think about where it puts the most pressure on the story. For descriptive context, ask: How much does your particular audience need to feel situated and at what point does it become superfluous? Use descriptive context as grounding: show where your characters are in relative space (staging), make obvious transitions and utilize space breaks, signpost time and place at the beginnings of sentences rather than at the end, etc.

28.

Here's an alternate way to think about plot (call it the *What would Alice Munro do?* method). First, identify all the scenes and potential scenes in your story. Then identify both the story arc and the character arc. What do these arcs suggest that the story is "about"? Compare these arcs to your list of scenes: Which scenes are necessary to the story arc? Which scenes are necessary to the character arc and make clear what the story is "about"? Now, here's where Munro comes in: imagine a new scene (or identify an existing or potential scene from your list) in which the causation that makes up the story arc *becomes* clear. In some/many Munro stories, the plot is still a plot of causation, but instead of the story being propelled forward by wondering what the character will cause to happen next, the story is propelled forward by wondering how what happens is connected to what happened before. In other words, the plot's causation isn't clear until the story jumps forward or backward to the point in time at which the causation becomes clear to the character. The character arc reveals the story arc, rather than the other way around.

For example, say we have a scene where a young girl witnesses her father killing a stray cat. Then a scene where the girl is a married woman and her husband refuses to let them take in a stray cat. Finally a scene where the woman is divorced and is out with her daughter, who is engaged to a boy with a cat. In the third scene, the woman comes to realize that the various scenes have led to each other, though they seemed discrete and separate events at the time. Surely her father killing a stray cat didn't lead to her husband refusing to take in a stray cat, which didn't lead to her daughter getting engaged to a boy with a cat. But— the woman now sees as she dines with her daughter—the attitudes toward a cat are both what drew her to her husband and made her divorce him, and perhaps also what drew her daughter to the boy, on some deep level. It might not even be so to the daughter, but the woman realizes that these events are how she has framed the boy, why she likes and approves of him, and why she hopes her daughter will not repeat her mistakes.

The above is a kind of Alice Munro "plot." Alternatively, someone like a Charles Dickens might link these events more directly. (The result of two different audiences with different expectations.) In the Dickens model, the cat might be a neighborhood cat, and the father killing the stray cat might lead to the girl secretly feeding stray cats, which end up breeding the cat the husband later refuses to take in—and that may be the exact moment that the girl, now a woman, divorces the husband, and why she eventually pushes her daughter to judge a man by his attitude toward cats. This all makes the action much more directly causally linked.

Does your story follow one of these models? Or another model? The "Charles Dickens" model might be more familiar—in the example above, it's basically the fairy tale model. For now, try to work your scenes into the Munro model. What does that do for your story? How does it change the audience?

29.

Research something fact-based or theory-based or historical, etc., and add at least ten "facts" (or statements of information) from your research that seem relevant to the thematic content of your story. Let the real world in. Maybe one of your characters is interested in the subject, or your protagonist goes to a museum or is handed a flyer or receives a mysterious phone call, or whatever. "Nonfiction" information, from research, can help get across the theme and focus the audience (provide to a certain audience the sense that it is learning something, while to another a sense of insiderness). Research can create interest and investment in a different way than stakes or conflict or so on. For example, in the novel *The Quick and the Dead*, by Joy Williams, environmental facts and theories get across the theme and character and give an immediate sense of who the ideal audience is.

30.

Go paragraph by paragraph and try to get each paragraph to answer at least *one* question that the story has already brought up, and also pose at least *two* more questions, until the climax.

31.

Revise your story so that it takes place in exactly three scenes (plus some narrative summary) OR exactly four scenes (plus narrative summary). Maybe you need to combine scenes, or add scenes. Maybe backstory moves into dialogue, or you add a flashback. Do whatever you need to do to make the draft work as a story. Your goal here is to hew strictly either to the three-act structure or to kishotenketsu. What do you learn by following the model so closely? What do you gain from freeing yourself again?

32.

Add a clock to the story—something that starts at the beginning of the story and counts down to the end. For example, Nana has two weeks to live. Or Mrs. Dalloway is going to throw a party. It is common for either the clock or its completion to be out of a character's control. Why do you think this is?

33.

The power of metaphor, like the power of a joke, is cultural. A metaphor is where a character meets the world—a specific character and a specific world—and translates the experience for the audience. An Asian American character comparing chopsticks to two snakes in her hand, for example, is not for an Asian American audience. Whom does the metaphor serve? What exactly is it translating? Go through your manuscript and interrogate each metaphor for whether it is relevant to the character, world, and audience. What shared context is necessary for the metaphor to work? Does it do the job better than a concrete description would?

34.

Below is a brief style guide mostly descending from Western, Hemingway-influenced conventions. Other traditions have different styles. Salman Rushdie, for example, seems firmly within a wordier tradition that Hemingway does not belong to. Hélène Cixous famously rejected masculine stylistic values. Style is clearly raced, gendered, etc. I am focusing here on density of sound and repurposing language.

- Nouns and verbs often do more direct work, with regard to meaning, than adjectives and especially adverbs.
- Consonants have more sonic impact than vowels.
- Hard consonants (e.g. *k*) have a different sonic impact than soft consonants (e.g. *g*). Hard consonants then might be more useful for, say, a fight scene, while soft consonants might be more useful for, say, a romantic interlude.
- Keep track of stressed and unstressed syllables. Stressed syllables have more sonic impact. More stresses than unstresses in a sentence might be useful for sentences meant to convey impact ("She pushed her back and kissed her hard" vs. "She maneuvered her over to the wall and kissed her on the lips"). More unstresses might usefully convey other things, such as hesitation ("She wiggled a little bit and tried uncomfortably to return the kisses").
- One-syllable nouns, verbs, and adjectives are usually stressed. It's easy to stack stresses this way (e.g. "The small red bird bit her thumb hard"). One-syllable words are often more familiar to a broader audience than longer words, and this too can be an advantage for some. On the other hand, the right word is the right word.

- A sentence that ends in a stressed syllable ends with a stronger sonic impact. It also draws out the pause between it and a new sentence that starts with a stressed syllable. ("She did. I did" vs. "She didn't. And I didn't.") Either can be used to your advantage, one to emphasize and one perhaps to cast doubt, for example. ("No one could ever hurt her" vs. "No one could hurt her ever.")
- Pay attention to sound and even let sound help select the next words. (I was going to write "let sound help determine the next words," but "select" carries through the *s* and *l* and adds a *c* sound that is echoed in "next.")
- Look for every time you use the word "was" or "is" and make sure it adds more than the alternatives. A lot of this has to do with using the right action verb. This will also help make your sentences active (a cultural value). It will also help with the next point.
- Use the simple form of the verb over the continuous ("She hummed Beethoven" vs. "She was humming Beethoven") unless accuracy is involved. This results in more stresses, fewer overall syllables, and more of a sense of action. Even though the two example sentences here can in many cases mean the same thing in a scene, the second conveys an ongoing state of

humming, a gerund, rather than an act. Also, individual actions have a different cultural value than simultaneous actions (as in "She swore and ran to the corner. Her backpack slammed against her back" vs. "She was swearing and running to the corner. Her backpack was slamming against her back") and can seem to carry more momentum to certain readers.

- Avoid introductory clauses (e.g. "Closing my eyes, I smiled") except when used as time or location markers, since those markers can be useful to situate the audience upfront ("At five o'clock," "When I got back from the store," "In the supermarket").

- Audience-wise, I would rather use common or colloquial words in new ways than use uncommon words in normal ways. I'd rather not send anyone to the dictionary, but I do like a turn of phrase.

- Avoid "begin" or "start" or any other intermediary actions ("I began to sing," "He started walking," "He got up from the couch and went to the door and opened it"). It might be more useful to ask your readers to do the intermediary work in their head. Again, though, this is cultural and is valued in certain cultures while seeming rushed or disjointed in others. ("I sing," "He walked," "He opened the door.")

A useful exception might be that Western audiences tend to associate a string of minute actions with tedium and even certain unhappy
moods, and you might use the description of
every single action to convey something like
depression.

• Really examine every time you use "look,"
"watch," "see," "feel," etc., and any other words
that "filter" (via John Gardner) the prose
through a perspective that is already well established. If we are in Jose's close-third perspective, for example, we don't need to know
that Jose looked at the clock in order to know
that he read the time. "The clock read 7:00"
does the job of implying that Jose looked at
the clock. This is an innocent example, but
sometimes the "filter" can obscure the object. Significant looks are cultural—I suspect
they come from watching screens. On screen
a significant look is something we can see the
specific details of. In prose, "She glared at his
mouth" cannot be used to take the place of
"She wanted to rip his mouth" or especially
"His mouth puckered stupidly."

• Alliteration and rhyme, which the West
seemed to value more in earlier literary work
(think Romantic poetry) now might make
us think of Dr. Seuss. Instead, you can get a

similar effect from consonance and assonance and slant rhyme, especially in the middles of words rather than at the beginnings or ends of them.

- In almost all instances, use "say" or "ask" instead of other dialogue tags. (See the chapter "'Pure Craft' Is a Lie")

- Patterns (and repetition) are most impactful where they are broken.

- Be purposeful. Be aware of the traditions you are working with. Everything is a decision. Make those decisions consciously and conscientiously.

WORKS OF FICTION REFERENCED

Anonymous. *Tales from the Thousand and One Nights* (New York: W. W. Norton, 2008), transl. Husain Haddawy.

Atkinson, Kate. *Life After Life* (New York: Reagan Arthur Books, 2013).

Austen, Jane. *Pride and Prejudice* (New York: W. W. Norton, 2016).

Bronte, Charlotte. *Jane Eyre* (New York: W. W. Norton, 2000).

Cervantes, Miguel de. *Don Quixote* (New York: Penguin Classics, 2003), transl. John Rutherford.

Chesnutt, Charles W. "Her Virginia Mammy." *The Wife of His Youth and other Stories of the Color Line* (Ann Arbor: University of Michigan Press, 1968).

Conrad, Joseph. *Heart of Darkness* (New York: W. W. Norton, 2016).

Cortázar, Julio. "The Island at Noon." *All Fires the Fire* (New York: Pantheon Books, 1973), transl. Suzanne Jill Levine.

Curious George (film) (Universal Pictures, 2006).

Fitzgerald, F. Scott. *The Great Gatsby* (New York: Scribner's, 1925).

Gonzales, Manuel. "Farewell, Africa." *The Miniature Wife* (New York: Riverhead Books, 2013).

Hagedorn, Jessica. *Dogeaters* (New York: Pantheon, 1990).

Kim, Richard. *The Martyred* (New York: George Braziller, 1964).

Kingston, Maxine Hong. *The Woman Warrior* (New York: Knopf, 1976).

Lahiri, Jhumpa. "Hell-Heaven." *Unaccustomed Earth* (New York: Knopf, 2008).

Le Guin, Ursula K. *A Wizard of Earthsea* (New York: Houghton Mifflin Harcourt, 2012 edition).

Lin, Grace. *Where the Mountain Meets the Moon* (New York: Little, Brown, 2009).

Mitchell, David. *Cloud Atlas* (New York: Random House, 2004).

Mo Yan. *Life and Death Are Wearing Me Out* (New York: Arcade, 2006), transl. Howard Goldblatt.

O'Connor, Flannery. "A Good Man Is Hard to Find." *A Good Man Is Hard to Find* (New York: Harcourt, Brace, 1955).

Okada, John. *No-No Boy* (Seattle: University of Washington Press, 1979 edition).

Wharton, Edith. *The Age of Innocence* (New York: D. Appleton and Company, 1920).

FURTHER BIBLIOGRAPHY

Achebe, Chinua. "An Image of Africa." *Hopes and Impediments* (New York: Anchor, 1990).

Adsit, Janelle, ed. *Critical Creative Writing* (New York: Bloomsbury Academic, 2018).

Adsit, Janelle. *Toward an Inclusive Creative Writing* (New York: Bloomsbury Academic, 2017).

Alison, Jane. *Meander, Spiral, Explode* (New York: Catapult, 2019).

Araki, Hirohiko. *Manga in Theory and Practice* (San Francisco: VIZ Media, LLC, 2017).

Aristotle. *On Poetics* (South Bend: St. Augustine's Press, 2002). Transl. Seth Benardete and Michael Davis.

Ball, Jesse. *Notes on My Dunce Cap* (New York: Pioneer Works, 2016).

Baxter, Charles. *Burning Down the House* (St. Paul, MN: Graywolf, 1997).

Bennett, Eric. *Workshops of Empire* (Iowa City: University of Iowa Press, 2015).

Bernays, Anne, and Pamela Painter, eds. *What If?* (New York: HarperCollins, 1990).

Booth, Wayne C. *The Rhetoric of Fiction* (Chicago: University of Chicago Press, 1961).

Boswell, Robert. *The Half-Known World* (St. Paul, MN: Graywolf, 2008).

Brooks, Peter. *The Melodramatic Imagination* (New Haven, CT: Yale University Press, 1976).

Burroway, Janet. *Writing Fiction: A Guide to Narrative Craft* (New York: Longman, 1982).

Campbell, Joseph. *The Hero with a Thousand Faces* (New York: Pantheon, 1949).

Carson, Anne. *Eros the Bittersweet* (Princeton, NJ: Princeton University Press, 1986).

Chatman, Seymour. *Story and Discourse: Narrative Structure in Fiction and Film* (Ithaca, NY: Cornell University Press, 1978).

Chee, Alexander. *How to Write an Autobiographical Novel* (New York: Mariner, 2018).

Chinweizu, Onwuchekwa Jemie, and Ihechukwu Madubuike. *Toward the Decolonization of African Literature* (Washington, D.C.: Howard University Press, 1983).

Cixous, Hélène. "The Laugh of the Medusa." *Signs* 1, no. 4 (Summer 1976): 875–93.

Cixous, Hélène. *Three Steps on the Ladder of Writing* (New York: Columbia University Press, 1993).

Cliff, Michelle. "A Journey into Speech." *The Land of Look Behind* (Ithaca, NY: Firebrand, 1985).

Cortázar, Julio. *Literature Class, Berkeley 1980* (New York: New Directions, 2017).

Donahue, James J., Jennifer Ann Ho, and Shaun Morgan, eds. *Narrative, Race, and Ethnicity in the United States* (Columbus: Ohio State University Press, 2017).

Feris, Wendy B. *Ordinary Enchantments: Magical Realism and the Remystification of Narrative* (Nashville, TN: Vanderbilt University Press, 2004).

Forster, E. M. *Aspects of the Novel* (London: Edward Arnold, 1927).

Freire, Paulo. *Pedagogy of the Oppressed* (New York: Bloomsbury, 2014 thirtieth anniversary edition).

Gardner, John. *The Art of Fiction* (New York: Vintage, 2010 reissue edition).

Gornick, Vivian. *The Situation and the Story* (New York: FSG, 2002).

Gu, Ming Dong. *Chinese Theories of Fiction: A Non-Western Narrative System* (Albany, NY: SUNY Press, 2007).

Gu, Ming Dong. *Chinese Theories of Reading and Writing* (Albany, NY: SUNY Press, 2012).

Harding, Jennifer Riddle. "Narrating the Family in Charles W. Chesnutt's 'Her Virginia Mammy.'" Special issue, *Journal of Narrative Theory: Decolonizing Narrative Theory* 42, no. 3 (Fall 2012).

Highsmith, Patricia. *Plotting and Writing Suspense Fiction* (New York: Poplar Press, 1983).

hooks, bell. *Teaching to Transgress* (New York: Routledge, 1994).

Hurston, Zora Neale. "Characteristics of Negro Expression." Smithsonian Libraries African Art Index Project DSI. Reprint of the 1934 edition.

James, Henry. *The Art of the Novel* (New York: Scribner's, 1934).

Jen, Gish. *Tiger Writing* (Cambridge, MA: Harvard University Press, 2013).

Jin, Ha. *The Writer as Migrant* (Chicago: University of Chicago Press, 2009).

Kim, Elaine. *Asian American Literature* (Philadelphia: Temple University Press, 1982).

Kim, Sue J., ed. Special issue, *Journal of Narrative Theory: Decolonizing Narrative Theory* 42, no. 3 (Fall 2012).

King, Thomas. *The Truth about Stories: A Native Narrative* (Toronto: House of Anansi Press, 2003).

Kundera, Milan. *The Art of the Novel* (New York: Grove, 1988).

Lamott, Anne. *Bird by Bird* (New York: Pantheon, 1994).

Lear, Jonathan. *Love and Its Place in Nature* (New York: FSG, 1990).

Lerman, Liz, and John Borstel. *Liz Lerman's Critical Response Process* (Dance Exchange, 2003).

Livesey, Margot. *The Hidden Machinery* (Portland, OR: Tin House, 2017).

Lodge, David. *The Art of Fiction* (New York: Penguin, 1992).

Lorde, Audre. *Sister Outsider* (New York: Crossing Press, 1984).

Lowe, Lisa. *Immigrant Acts* (Durham, NC: Duke University Press, 1996).

Marzolph, Ulrich. "Making Sense of the Nights." *Narrative Culture* 1, no. 2 (2014).

McGurl, Mark. *The Program Era* (Cambridge, MA: Harvard University Press, 2011).

Morrison, Toni. *The Origin of Others* (Cambridge, MA: Harvard University Press, 2017).

Morrison, Toni. *Playing in the Dark* (Cambridge, MA: Harvard University Press, 1992).

Muller, Lauren, ed. *June Jordan's Poetry for the People* (New York: Routledge, 1995).

Mulvey, Laura. "Visual Pleasure and Narrative Cinema." *Screen* 16, no 3. (Autumn 1975): 6–18.

Mura, David. *A Stranger's Journey* (Athens: University of Georgia Press, 2018).

Nguyen, Viet Thanh. *Race and Resistance* (Oxford: Oxford University Press, 2002).

O'Connor, Flannery. *Mystery and Manners* (New York: FSG, 1969).

Ondaatje, Michael. *The Conversations: Walter Murch and the Art of Editing Film* (New York: Knopf, 2002).

Orner, Peter. *Am I Alone Here?* (New York: Catapult, 2016).

Pagh, Nancy, ed. *Write Moves* (Peterborough, ON: Broadview, 2016).

Pamuk, Orhan. *The Naïve and Sentimental Novelist* (Cambridge, MA: Harvard University Press, 2010).

Park, Chan E. "Poetics and Politics of Korean Oral Tradition in a Cross-Cultural Context." *World of Music* 45, no. 3 (2003): 91–103.

Percy, Benjamin. *Thrill Me* (St. Paul, MN: Graywolf, 2016).

Plaks, Andrew. "Towards a Critical Theory of Chinese Narrative." *Chinese Narrative: Critical and Theoretical Essays* (Princeton, NJ: Princeton University Press, 1977).

Pollack, David. *Reading Against Culture* (Ithaca, NY: Cornell University Press, 1992).

Prose, Francine. *Reading Like a Writer: A Guide for People Who Love Books and for Those Who Want to Write Them* (New York: HarperCollins, 2006).

Qian, Jianan. "The Moon Is Beautiful Tonight: On East Asian Narratives." *The Millions* (web). April 17, 2018.

Rankine, Claudia, ed. *The Racial Imaginary: Writers on Race in the Life of the Mind* (Albany, NY: Fence, 2015).

Rhodes, Jewell Parker. *Free Within Ourselves: Fiction Lessons for Black Authors* (New York: Main Street Books, 1999).

Ritter, Kelly, and Stephanie Vanderslice, eds. *Can It Really Be Taught? Resisting Lore in Creative Writing Pedagogy* (Portsmouth, NH: Boynton/Cook, 2007).

Tilley, Allen. *Plots of Time* (Gainesville: University Press of Florida, 1995).

Trinh T. Minh-ha. *Woman Native Other* (Bloomington: Indiana University Press, 1989).

Turchi, Peter. "Making the Most of a Writing Workshop; or: Out of the Workshop, into the Laboratory." peterturchi.com (web).

Turchi, Peter. *Maps of the Imagination: The Writer as Cartographer* (San Antonio, TX: Trinity University Press, 2004).

Vizenor, Gerald, ed. *Survivance: Narratives of Native Presence* (Lincoln: University of Nebraska Press, 2008).

Vonnegut, Kurt. "The Shapes of Stories." YouTube.com (lecture) (web).

Wang, Dorothy. *Thinking Its Presence* (Stanford, CA: Stanford University Press, 2014).

Whitehead, Harry. "The Programmatic Era: Creative Writing as Cultural Imperialism." *ariel* 47, no. 1–2 (January–April 2016).

Yu, Anthony C. "History, Fiction, and the Reading of Chinese Narrative." *Chinese Literature: Essays, Articles, Reviews (CLEAR)* 10, no. 1/2 (July 1988): 1–19.

ACKNOWLEDGMENTS

This book began in the classroom in 2011, in the safety of failing together. My most heartfelt thanks go to my students, who consistently invest in our shared vulnerability. I put most of this book together in Korea a year after my wife's death. Language was difficult, and language was everything.

Thank you to the editors who believed in the importance of this work, especially Phong Nguyen, who gave me space and freedom at *Pleiades*, and Kat Chow. Thanks to the writers who built the foundation for this work and to those who will take the work further than I have. Always thanks to Kirstin Chen, who reads everything. Thanks to Nami Mun, who changed my teaching with a single sentence I have never forgotten.

Thank you to heroes Joy Castro, Jennine Capó Crucet, Beth Nguyen, Alexandra Kleeman, Tiphanie Yanique, Megan Stielstra, Leni Zumas, Roxane Gay, and everyone else who wanted to see this book before it existed.

Thank you to my mentors and friends at Emerson

College and the University of Houston. Thank you to Tin House and Kundiman and Inprint and Grub Street and the UH Asian American Studies Center and the Coe English Department and the many other institutions that let me teach differently from what is "normal."

Many endless thanks to the people at Catapult who made this book a book, most especially Megha Majumdar, Julie Buntin, Alisha Gorder, Katie Boland, Megan Fishmann, and Rachel Fershleiser. Thanks forever to Ayesha Pande, my dream agent. To my readers, thank you, so much, for offering such support and love. If this book has a long life, it will be because of you.

MATTHEW SALESSES is the author of three novels, *Disappear Doppelgänger Disappear*, *The Hundred-Year Flood*, and *I'm Not Saying, I'm Just Saying*, and a forthcoming essay collection. He has taught at Coe College, the Ashland MFA program, the Tin House and Kundiman summer workshops, and writing centers like Grub Street and Inprint, among others. He has edited fiction for *Gulf Coast*, *Redivider*, and *The Good Men Project* and has written about craft and creative writing workshops for venues like NPR's *Code Switch*, *The Millions*, *Electric Literature*, and *Pleiades*. He was adopted from Korea and currently lives in Iowa.